POPE
FRANCIS
AND THE
PARISH

POPE FRANCIS AND THE PARISH

THE JOY OF THE GOSPEL COMES ALIVE

Kevin E. McKenna

FOREWORD BY John Stowe, OFM Conv
Bishop of Lexington

Paulist Press
New York / Mahwah, NJ

Cover image by Svetlana Vorotniak / Shutterstock.com
Cover and book design by Lynn Else

Library of Congress Cataloging-in-Publication Data
Names: McKenna, Kevin E., 1950– author.
Title: Pope Francis and the parish : the joy of the gospel comes alive / Kevin E McKenna.
Description: New York : Paulist Press, [2022] | Includes bibliographical references. | Summary: "A practical guide to parish reform as envisioned by Pope Francis"— Provided by publisher.
Identifiers: LCCN 2022000069 (print) | LCCN 2022000070 (ebook) | ISBN 9780809156009 (paperback) | ISBN 9780809187584 (ebook)
Subjects: LCSH: Church renewal—Catholic Church. | Pastoral theology—Catholic Church. | Evangelistic work—Catholic Church. | Catholic Church. Pope (2013– : Francis). Evangelii gaudium. | Church work with the poor—Catholic Church.
Classification: LCC BX1746 .M38 2022 (print) | LCC BX1746 (ebook) | DDC 262/.02—dc23/eng/20220526
LC record available at https://lccn.loc.gov/2022000069
LC ebook record available at https://lccn.loc.gov/2022000070

ISBN 978-0-8091-5600-9 (paperback)
ISBN 978-0-8091-8758-4 (e-book)

Published by Paulist Press
997 Macarthur Boulevard
Mahwah, New Jersey 07430
www.paulistpress.com

Printed and bound in the
United States of America

In loving gratitude to the Cathedral Community in
Rochester, New York, who eagerly taught me
to celebrate *The Joy of the Gospel*

Let us go forth, then, let us go forth to offer everyone the life of Jesus Christ.

Pope Francis

CONTENTS

FOREWORD

The appearance of the relatively unknown Jorge Mario Bergoglio on the balcony of St. Peter's on the night of March 13, 2013, was unforgettable for many of us. Simply dressed, looking a bit nervous, the hitherto Cardinal Archbishop of Buenos Aires managed to silence the massive crowd gathered below when he asked for their prayers and requested a blessing over himself before he gave his blessing to the world. The first Latin American and the first Jesuit to be elected to the Chair of Peter, he both delighted and intrigued when he chose to become the first pope named Francis. His origins, the choice of his name, and his simple greeting of *buona sera* before introducing himself as the one whom the cardinals selected from the ends of the earth to become Bishop of Rome all revealed more about him and the direction he envisioned for the Church than anyone could have grasped at the time.

So inspired by his story, his smile, and his evident humility, I was personally reenergized in ministry and in my hope for a renewed Church after it had been so long immersed in scandals and in depressing statistics. He reminded me not only of the directive to "rebuild the church" that Francis of Assisi heard spoken from the image of the crucifix in the Church of San Damiano, but also of Francis's lesser-known admonition to his friars, how upon entering a new place they must preach before they ever utter a word or they would really have nothing to say. Pope Francis preached when he boarded a bus with other cardinals, when he paid his own hotel bill, when he celebrated Mass in the Vatican's parish church of St. Ann and in so many gestures that have often resonated more than any homily or even encyclicals and apostolic exhortations.

But the pope's writings, combined with the witness of his genuineness, are indeed kerygmatic. Fr. Kevin McKenna, author, and rector of Rochester's Sacred Heart Cathedral, has captured the authenticity of this pope and the Franciscan joy that radiates from all that he says and does. Like his namesake, this Francis not only prioritizes the poor and marginalized, he is able to face an often brutal and dehumanizing world with the same joy exhibited by the Troubadour from Assisi. As a canonist and theologian, Fr. McKenna has previously demonstrated his gift for sharing the great riches of the Church's theology, social teaching, and even canon law in an easily digestible manner so that they can be useful for the life of the Church and for building up the kingdom of God. McKenna shows that the Second Vatican Council, the transformative way its vision was implemented in Latin America, the Ignatian charism of discernment, and of finding God in all things are all evident in the person of Francis and were presented to the universal Church in his first apostolic exhortation, *The Joy of the Gospel*.

Using his own parish as a workshop, Fr. McKenna shows that the gospel is indeed contagious when it is lived and practiced with joy. He demonstrates that missionary disciples can really read the signs of the times, discern how to respond in the light of the gospel, and do so. He describes a Church that is not bound by the way things have always been done but freed by accepting tradition as a cherished gift that has been handed on and will be handed on to the future. With Pope Francis and his parishioners, Fr. McKenna dreams of a world overcoming the globalization of indifference and working together to preserve the planet, our common home. Now, with a global synod underway in the Church, Sacred Heart Cathedral is giving us a foretaste and preview of how a synodal church might look and function.

Exactly two years into this dynamic pontificate, I received a call from the Apostolic Nuncio informing me that I had been selected to be the bishop of Lexington. I barely heard those shocking words when they were immediately followed by the question, "Do you accept?" Before I could even consider an answer, one came forth spontaneously from my mouth, "I love Pope Francis and would do whatever he asks." Sadly, I have learned that not everyone in the Church shares that love for our joyful yet determined pontiff. Even more disturbing is that the Church in the United States, which ought to be well prepared to engage in this fresh application of Vatican II ecclesiology, is hardly enthusiastic about doing so. I have heard many voices lamenting the failure of the U.S. bishops to lead the Church with the priorities of Pope Francis or even sowing division among the faithful about their orthodoxy or legitimacy.

I found a wonderful template for my mission diocese in *The Joy of the Gospel*; it forms the centerpiece of our pastoral plan in Lexington. In the pages that follow, Fr. Kevin McKenna reminds us that the U.S. Church is made up principally of parishes and how the parish is meant to be the primary vehicle for evangelization. Our parishes are fertile grounds for planting the seeds of gospel joy and for forming the missionary disciples who will be eager to rebuild the Church, breathe new life into its stagnation, redeem its brokenness and sinfulness, and orient it toward Jesus, whose compassionate mercy most perfectly reveals the face of his Father. May these pages help the reader to catch the contagious joy of the gospel, be moved to encounter Christ among those in the margins, and become ever more committed to God's vision of a new heaven and a new earth.

† *John Stowe, OFM Conv*
Bishop of Lexington, Kentucky

PREFACE

On November 24, 2013, Pope Francis issued an apostolic exhortation, a typical papal teaching document that popes have used to disseminate teachings or instructions to the worldwide Catholic community, usually encouraging and promoting a particular virtue or activity. Like many other exhortations, it was issued following a meeting of the Synod of Bishops. But in dramatic ways *The Joy of the Gospel* was unique. In style it used easy language and vivid images. In vision it was clearly charting a new course for the Church.

The significance of the document was immediately identified in the Catholic world. A reporter compared this document to the Dr. Martin Luther King Jr's "I Have A Dream" speech.[1] The pope, as Dr. King, had done for civil rights, was proclaiming his vision, in this case a dream for the Church. Francis had just become pope in March of that year. The world was enthralled and fascinated by the stories that were told about his career before the papacy, including his birth in Argentina, his humble beginnings, his Jesuit training and experience, his time as archbishop in Buenos Aires, and, particularly, the simplicity of his lifestyle. People were also curious and delighted in the narrative events of the first days of his pontificate: he emerged on the loggia of the Vatican shortly after his election with a simple and humble request for prayers from the faithful as he began his papal ministry; appearing in St. Peter's Square not wearing the traditional mozzetta, or short red cape, clothed simply in a white papal cassock; his drive back to the residence of Santa Marta with the cardinals, not in a papal limousine but on a bus with the cardinals who had elected him; paying his bill at the hotel where he had stayed before the conclave, and his desire to live at the Santa Marta residence, rather than the papal palace. These and other stories that circulated stimulated much curiosity and conjecture about his agenda for the Church.

The Joy of the Gospel reveals Jorge Bergoglio's past as well as his imagination, and how his own pastoral experiences could propel the Church in a new direction with a different focal point. He craves a Church more outward looking and not so self-absorbed. He hungers for a Church not so absorbed in its inner life, defending doctrine, but would instead turn its gaze to addressing the messiness of today's world. In this he would be returning to the insights that had been provided by the bishops of the Second Vatican Council in such documents as *Lumen Gentium* and *Gaudium et Spes*. These documents had also invited the Church to a more global perspective, aligning itself with the joys and sufferings of the world in which the Church found itself. This exhortation was looking back to that vision and looking toward the future in hope.

Such a vision would require a method: the need to "accompany." Pope Francis was looking at a missionary thrust, for a discipleship that would involve going forth for all the followers of Jesus as missionary disciples, sharing the gospel through a joyful acceptance of the Lord Jesus, which would impact their message that was shared—"good news"—not be proclaimed by what he would term "sourpusses" but rather be a people so filled with the joy of Jesus and his message that they would bring joy to the people that they encountered. The format and style for this evangelization would be a journey—people walking together and listening to each other. The vision would not be of harsh or strident confrontation, polemics, or apologetics. Rather, there was a "softer" approach envisioned, of spreading the gospel by a life that had been touched in a powerful way by Jesus Christ, and an encounter that had changed the person so completely and thoroughly that they could not resist living the new life and sharing it more by example than words with the people they accompanied.

The missionary impulse was also to be seen as focused on the poor.

From the beginning of his pontificate, Pope Francis gave indication that this would be an important, if not the most important, focus of his ministry. "I desire to have a Poor Church of the Poor" he would proclaim within the first days in his Petrine ministry. *The Joy of the Gospel* is consumed with chapter and verse about the needs of the poor and the concern that the Church must have for them. It is also focused on the structural changes that need to take place within the world economy, which the pope pushes to change in its emphasis, believing that it does great harm to those who live on the margins of society. The members of the Christian household must walk with the poor, share in their struggles, and work to raise the economic life of everyone. He disdains a "trickle-down economy," which teaches that as the wealthier get wealthier, the wealth will "trickle down" to those who experience poverty. In true equality we recognize our codependence.

The Joy of the Gospel demands a greater decentralization within the Church, a veering away from a "top-down" approach to ministry. Although accepting a hierarchical structure, he would like to see better collaboration between the bishops and the curia. He encourages the curia to a listening posture with the bishops and their diocesan concerns, rather than taking a dominating role. Episcopal conferences, regional gatherings of bishops, should exercise a more prominent role in the universal Church, which he has attempted to implement, for example, by including references to their documents on ecology in his encyclical on the environment, *Laudato Si'* (On Care for Our Common Home).

The Church is called to celebrate more emphatically the gifts of the entire people of God. Their participation should not only be welcomed but encouraged.

Pope Francis summons the Church to a fresh mindset, a reenvisioning and reorientation of the Church to serve today's needs. He identifies new styles of pastoral leadership and priorities. *The Joy of the Gospel* is a revolutionary document in its tone, direction, and scope. To be a joyful community of believers, completely unafraid of new opportunities that require change, is provocative and exciting. It must take on the status quo and must overcome the complacent attitude that always responds to innovation: "We have always done it this way." "There are ecclesial structures which can hamper efforts at evangelization, yet even good structures are only helpful when there is life constantly driving, sustaining and assessing them" (*Evangelii Gaudium* 26).[2] This is particularly important for the structures of pastoral ministry that lend themselves easily to routine and standard-ized procedures. In a parish, we can easily succumb to both a daily and weekend routine. Our liturgies are rituals, celebrated at a certain time with a certain structure. We can easily approach the other aspects of pastoral ministry in a similar way: at a certain time with a certain structure. When we prepare a couple for marriage, we always prepare them with the same programs and the same recommenda-tions for a successful marriage without adjusting our responses to the two unique individuals with their history and relationship to faith and the Church. The Second Vatican Council document on the lit-urgy reminds us, "Pastors of souls must therefore realize that, when the liturgy is celebrated, their obligation goes farther than simply ensuring that the laws governing valid and lawful celebrations are observed. They must ensure that the faithful take part fully aware of what they are doing" (*Sacrosanctum Concilium* 11).[3] *The Joy of the Gospel* proclaims an "ecclesial renewal" that demands that we look carefully and honestly at what we are doing; to see more clearly the evangelizing opportunities that are latent in each sacred act and the pastoral tasks we are charged with; to be unafraid of possible new ways of living the gospel and vibrant new ways of thinking about the Church. We are to avoid the temptations of clericalism with a renewed appreciation of the charisms of the entire people of God, available—if they are permitted to contribute their talents.

Pope Francis has no patience for people who just moan and grouse, who are "tempted to find excuses and complain." There are many, he says, who seem to live lives "more like Lent than Easter."

He calls for a hope-filled, positive, and vitalized view of the Church that is engaged with the world.

An "ecclesial renewal that cannot be deferred" demands a structural change that is founded on the same vision that was a part of the renewal of the Second Vatican Council. "Every renewal of the church essentially consists in an increase of fidelity to her own calling...Christ summons the church, as she goes her pilgrim way, to that continual reformation of which she always has need, insofar as she is a human institution here on earth" (*Unitatis Redintegratio* 6).[4] So true also for personal renewal, which Francis insists comes only after a personal encounter with Jesus Christ. Without such a relationship at the center of the Christian's life, the commitment to any kind of evangelization is useless. There is a great need to be constantly renewed in the experience of savoring Christ's friendship and his message.

"Nobody can go off to battle unless he is fully convinced of victory beforehand." The Christian missionary, filled with a confidence that comes from abiding in Jesus Christ, is assured of ultimate triumph in the proclamation of the gospel. Such victory is not dependent on his or her own efforts but by working with a community of disciples, motivated by a personal relationship with Jesus and the promises of the gospel. Such an approach is unstoppable!

It is hard to gage the impact of any one papal encyclical or exhortation. It is clear, however, that Pope Francis has vigorously pushed the Church along the lines promoted by this exhortation. We have forgotten, for a variety of reasons, the schematic, strategy, and vision, contained in *The Joy of the Gospel*. Various commentators have lamented the failure of the Church at all levels to move on, without completely digesting the content, thrust, and vision of the exhortation. Some have speculated that the clergy sexual abuse crisis might have seen a better outcome if the insights of *The Joy of the Gospel* had been heeded. One can only speculate on the reasons why the exhortation did not, in some quarters, have a deeper influence. Perhaps the renewed ecclesiology went too far. Perhaps it required, as the pope himself says in the exhortation, going beyond "what we have always done" and too big a shove beyond complacency. Perhaps the economic critique provided by Pope Francis was too harsh or challenging, especially for Western minds. Perhaps an approach to the poor that went beyond more charity to a more thoughtful and courageous piercing of structural evils that caused the poverty was beyond what anyone was willing to confront. Or perhaps quite simply, due to the pace of change, there was not enough time to digest the agenda. Yet even a casual read of the exhortation shows continuity in Pope Francis's pontificate, for example, the need to immerse oneself in the love of Jesus Christ in any evangelization effort; the synodal approach of participation and walking together, in the manner in which succeeding universal synods proceeded with an encouragement of honest participation; the impact of economic disparities on the poor, even beginning before the exhortation with his comments about "a poor Church for the poor." At the conclave he had been requested by a fellow cardinal immediately after his election "not to forget the poor." Already as archbishop of Buenos Aires he had sent priests to the poorer barrios.

With the promulgation of *The Joy of the Gospel*, Pope Francis was not only providing the Church with a road map to follow, but he would be following the road map himself.

The "ecclesial renewal that cannot be deferred" is a "missionary impulse" that "transforms everything…an effort to make them [structures of the Church] more mission-oriented, to make ordinary pastoral activity on every level more inclusive and open, to inspire in pastoral workers a constant desire to go forth" (*EG* 27). How does such a renewal take place? How can this required renewal take shape in the most basic pastoral structure, the parish? More fundamentally, does the parish still serve a purpose? If it does, what is it?

The parish must live up to its potential. "The parish is not an outdated institution; precisely because it possesses great flexibility, it can assume quite different contours depending on the openness and missionary creativity of the pastor and community" (*EG* 28).

Unless refocused, the parish risks becoming ineffective. "If the parish proves capable of self-renewal and constant adaptivity, it continues to be 'the Church living in the midst of the homes of her sons and daughters (*Christfidelis Laici*)" (*EG* 28). The commitment to missionary discipleship is the only way to a reinvigorating of the ecclesial structures in the Church, and it can transform everything.

The Second Vatican Council's Decree on the Missionary Activity of the Church, *Ad Gentes*, declared the Church must always be outwardly directed in mission. "The Church on earth is by its very nature missionary since, according to the plan of the Father, it has its origin in the mission of the Son and the holy Spirit" (*Ad Gentes* 2).[5] "Mission" could no longer be something that ordained and religious accomplished by leaving their native countries and traveling to far-away places proclaiming the gospel. Every Christian and Christian community must assimilate the missionary impulse to see where the gospel must be proclaimed. Pope John Paul II once shared with a group of bishops, "All renewal in the Church must have mission as its goal if it is not to fall prey to a kind of ecclesial introversion" (*EG* 27).

The parish must be continuously creative and adaptive to new missionary opportunities. It is the locus and focus where most Catholics come in contact with the living Church:

> The parish is the presence of the Church in a given territory, an environment for hearing God's word, for growth in the Christian life, for dialogue, proclamation, charitable outreach, worship and celebration. In all its activities the parish encourages and trains its members to be evangelizers. It is a community of communities, a sanctuary where the thirsty come to drink in the midst of their journey; and a center of constant missionary outreach. (*EG* 28)

The present work is a reflection on the apostolic exhortation *The Joy of the Gospel* and how the parish can respond to the vision of Pope Francis to embark on *"the ecclesial renewal that cannot be deferred."*

We will use as reference an urban cathedral parish in a mid-sized city adapting its service model from a blue-collar, middle-class population to an urban poor neighborhood within a short period of time. I have served as pastor for this faith community since 2008.

The area had been largely vacated by employees of Eastman Kodak, a major film and camera manufacturer, who left after a drastic downsizing. Many Anglos have remained in the neighborhood, and many former residents come back for weekend Mass. The parish neighborhood is now 41 percent African American and 19 percent Hispanic. A substantial influx of refugees in the last several years, primarily from Myanmar (Burma) and Nepal, has added additional diversity.

The parish gradually realized its need to thoroughly adapt to its surroundings and redirect its ministerial energies in a more concentrated missionary direction. *The Joy of the Gospel* has been an important guide in this journey.

This work is not a manual for implementation of the missionary discipleship proposed by Pope Francis. There were and will continue to be many mistakes and false starts in implementing the vision of the *Joy of the Gospel*. But it demonstrates how one parish has attempted to work out the "missionary impulse" and the resulting "joy of the gospel" it experienced. It also tried to learn from its many mistakes.

There is an expression used in some AA gatherings—take what you need and disregard the rest. So too, with this in mind, we can hope that some of these reflections can help in the road to the renewal that cannot be deferred.

ACKNOWLEDGMENTS

Pope Francis, in *The Joy of the Gospel*, speaks of the call of every community to obey the Lord's call to "go forth from our own comfort zone in order to reach the 'peripheries' in need of the light of the Gospel." It has been a blessing to pastor a faith community that has willingly embraced a Church that is "bruised, hurting and dirty." Their missionary impulse has become a driving force to provide the "strength, light and consolation born of friendship with Jesus Christ." For this opportunity, I am most grateful.

My appreciation and thanks go to Fr. Isaac Slater, OCSO, and Mark Hare for their generous labor in reviewing the manuscript and offering kind wisdom and helpful suggestions.

Chapter 1

FOUNDATIONS FOR ECCLESIAL RENEWAL

I dream of a "missionary option," that is, a missionary
impulse capable of transforming everything.

Evangelii Gaudium 27

The Joy of the Gospel contains both practical vision and wisdom about
themes close to Pope Francis's heart: personal conversion to Jesus
Christ; the call to a missionary spirituality and discipleship; gospel-
based ecclesial renewal; the rediscovery of importance of the poor
for the Church and a Church that is poor with the development of
a compassionate economic system that takes cognizance of the well-
being of all members of society.

The vision of this document did not form in a vacuum. It is the
culmination of the pope's Jesuit vocation and training; the variety of
his experiences as a Jesuit priest, including his time as a provincial
superior; his service as an auxiliary bishop and archbishop of Buenos
Aires, Argentina; his work with the Latin American Bishops' Conference, especially the Fifth General Conference at Aparecida (2007)
where he played a key role; as well as the documents of the Second
Vatican Council.

It is beyond the scope of this work to offer a comprehensive
analysis of each of these catalysts, but a brief survey of some of these

1

biographical details can serve as a helpful hermeneutic in understanding the pastoral themes of *The Joy of the Gospel.*

Jorge Bergoglio's vocation and formation as a Jesuit was a key determinant of his spiritual awakening. The Jesuits were the largest religious community in Bergoglio's native Argentina and the largest Catholic religious order in the world, with more than seventeen thousand members located in more than one hundred countries. "Jorge's formation led him to draw deep from the wells of Ignatian spirituality and Jesuit history, developing a vision of formation that he would implement as a novice master and provincial."[1] This formation would include the Spiritual Exercises of the founder, St. Ignatius Loyola (1491–1556), a set of Christian meditations developed during Ignatius's own conversion after he had been seriously injured by a cannonball in Pamplona while in battle. The Exercises, over several weeks, provide opportunities for extended periods of silent prayer. The aim of the intense prayer is growth in relationship with Jesus Christ and a vibrant commitment to discipleship. As a Jesuit, Bergoglio would publicly commit himself to a life unencumbered by a concern for possessions, in order to be totally available to serve others and free for mission and service where most needed. Besides the commitment to a certain poverty of spirit, Chris Lowney describes the significance of *humility* in formation: "Ignatius wanted Jesuits to be humble because Jesus, their role model, was humble. But he also understood how ambition and political infighting can shred organizational morale....So he was trying to rein in the human tendency to stroke one's ego by seeking status, power and advancement."[2]

Jorge Bergoglio's leadership talents were swiftly identified by his superiors. He was appointed for a six-year term as provincial in 1973. In this capacity he was responsible for the Jesuits within his province (a specific geographical region of Jesuits within one country). Dushan Croos defines this role: "The principal task of the Provincial is to meet each of the Jesuits of his Province and those working in his Province at least once every year for a conversation known as the Account of Conscience, as he makes a Visitation to each community and each Jesuit work."[3] This conversation is helpful to the provincial in planning assignments for the individual Jesuit. "He should give the Superior any information which would better inform the choice of mission, without trying to convince the Superior of where he should go or should not be sent, unless he is asking to go 'on the missions' or be given a particularly difficult task, such as that of novice master."[4] Particularly important in this discernment is obedience, but it is an "obedience" born of a trust in the provincial by the Jesuit, "that he is seeking God's will as well as the needs of the Church, of the Society and of this particular Jesuit."[5]

Ivereigh identifies growing awareness in Bergoglio's theological thinking as provincial: the significance of *pueblo fiel*, "the theology of the people,"[6] a natural development from the Second Vatican Council and "The People of God." "The *pueblo fiel* were both vaccine and antidote, the hermeneutic of a true reform."[7]

Such a realization moved him to action: he redeployed Jesuits to outlying areas to evangelize the poor—"to send out to the periphery those who had grown too comfortable in the residences."[8]

His time as provincial was not easy. As he affirmed in an early interview after becoming pope, he now believes that he was too young to be appointed to such a position. "My style of government as a Jesuit at the beginning had many faults....I was only 36 years old. That was crazy. I had to deal with difficult situations, and I made my decisions abruptly and by myself....It was my authoritarian way of making decisions that created problems."[9]

Formed as a Jesuit, Bergoglio was immersed in a lifestyle that underscored the eminence of prayer wedded to leadership. For the sake of integrity, any changes he wished to see in the Jesuit community had to start with himself. As Lowney observes, "You cannot lead others unless you lead yourself, so leaders dig deeply into themselves, confront their flaws, and ultimately, achieve peaceful acceptance of themselves and the unique role they play in the world."[10] Thus, his approach to leadership as a follower of Jesus, greatly impacted by his Jesuit experience, pushed him into the world with all its complexities. He became more aware of the poor and the peripheries as an important mission of the Jesuit community as well as the wider Church. He embraced the *pueblo fiel,* a "bottom-up" ecclesiology.

Jorge Bergoglio was named a bishop in 1992. It is unusual but not unheard of for a Jesuit to be named a bishop, as Dushan Croos explains, "because they vow not to seek honors and offices in the Church and to resist them as far as possible. It is only when the Pope truly stresses that a particular Jesuit is needed as a bishop that a Jesuit will accept the nomination."[11]

After serving first as an auxiliary, or assisting, bishop to the archbishop of Buenos Aires, he himself was named archbishop in 1997. Ivereigh describes his typical approach to leadership and honors: "He refused a ceremony of installation and reception and gave no interviews. He didn't even want new clothes. He asked the nuns who cooked in the curia to adjust Quarracino's [his immediate predecessor] purple-piped black tunics to his size."[12] His lifestyle would not change with his new position. "He turned down the official archbishop's residence—a seigneurial affair fifteen miles from the center in the leafy suburb of Olivos, close to the presidential mansion—as well as the official limousine and chauffeur. Instead he moved into the modern archdiocesan office building known as the curia, next to the cathedral....Inside the curia he refused the elegant and spacious archbishop's office in order to occupy a small office on the same floor with a desk and three chairs."[13]

In 2001, Pope John Paul II named him a cardinal. His response to this honor was typical of his personality and Jesuit roots. Ivereigh quotes a conversation Bergoglio had with writer and friend of Bergoglio, Elisabetta Pique: "I pray about it [elevation to the cardinalate], speak to the Lord about it, I plea on behalf of the diocese....In Gospel terms, every elevation implies a descent; you have to abase yourself in order to serve better."[14] Recognizing his own faults positively affected his leadership style. Good leaders, with a healthy sense of themselves, flaws and all, can work collaboratively: "They do not live for themselves alone but transcend themselves to serve others. The wisdom and energy generated from their self-knowledge isn't bottled up but radiates outward."[15]

Pope Francis's style of governing, demonstrated in *The Joy of the Gospel*, can be summarized succinctly: "He focuses on one priority only: he is a follower of Jesus, and his Jesuit formation helps him follow Jesus more closely, end of story."[16]

In addition to his Jesuit formation, Jorge Bergoglio was deeply affected and formed by the Second Vatican Council (1962–65). Convoked by Pope John XXIII, it was to be a Council with a benign face. "The Church has always opposed...errors. Frequently she has condemned with the greatest severity," Pope John XXIII preached before the Council began. "Nowadays, however, the Spouse of Christ prefers to make use of the medicine of mercy rather than that of severity. She considers that she meets the needs of the present day by demonstrating the validity of her teaching rather than by condemnation."[17] The Council was also to look with optimism at its relationship with the world. "We feel we must disagree with those prophets of gloom who are always forecasting disaster, as though the end of the world were at hand."[18]

Pope John XXIII, in calling for an ecumenical council, with his historian's eye and knowing the role of many prior councils, sensed its potential for needed Church reform. An important development in ecclesiology was the Church as the people of God. Bradford Hinze discusses the significant impact of the third chapter of the Council document *Lumen Gentium*: that *all* the baptized faithful are equal in dignity and freedom and destined for holiness. "This change introduced the possibility that the people of God motif would provide a framework for understanding the relationships of all groups in the Church."[19] This construct, from strong biblical roots, was a key interpretive lens for the Council. "The Christian community is a people with roots in the call of the Israelites—a community chosen and sent on pilgrimage in history....The people of God are commissioned to welcome those considered outsiders and strangers, reaching to all peoples created by God."[20] This archetype was fully assimilated by Bergoglio.

Another reference point, particularly esteemed by Pope Francis and frequently cited is Paul VI's apostolic exhortation *Evangelii Nuntiandi*, On Evangelization in the Modern World (1975), and its key premise: "Modern man listens more willingly to witnesses than to teachers and if he does listen to teachers, it is because they are witnesses" (no. 41).[21] As Ivereigh explains, this exhortation was Bergoglio's road map for reform. "*Evangelii Nuntiandi* would be Bergoglio's favorite Church document, the one he would cite throughout his time as provincial, rector, and later bishop."[22] In his pre-conclave address to the cardinals, Bergoglio made reference to Pope Paul VI and the "sweet and comforting joy of evangelizing."[23] After his election, he subsequently affirmed *Evangelii Nuntiandi* as "the greatest pastoral document ever written. Its great purpose was to reconcile eternal Church teaching with the diversity of cultures."[24]

Also influential to Bergoglio's theological and pastoral maturation were the meetings of the Latin American and Caribbean Episcopal Conference (CELAM), "the oldest and most highly developed transnational collegial body in the Church."[25] In 1967, Pope Paul VI issued the encyclical letter *Populorum Progressio*, On the Development of People, addressing the need to expand world economies to serve "the more and not the few." "The development of peoples has the Church's close attention, particularly the development of those peoples striving to escape from hunger, misery, endemic diseases and ignorance, of those who are looking for a wider share in the benefits of civilization and a more active improvement of their human qualities; of those who are aiming purposefully at their complete fulfillment" (*Populorum Progressio* 1).[26] The importance of the Church bringing the plight of developing nations to the attention of the wider Church and world came quite naturally from the Council just recently completed:

> Following on the Second Vatican Ecumenical Council
> a renewed consciousness of the demands of the Gospel
> makes it her duty to put herself at the service of all, to

help them grasp their serious problem in all its dimensions, and to convince them that solidarity in action at this turning point in human history is a matter of urgency. (no. 1)

The bishops' conference of Latin America met in Medellín, Colombia, in 1968 to scrutinize their relationship to the poor in light of Pope Paul's teachings and *Populorum Progressio*. Medellín reinforced the notion of the Church as the people of God, and the urgency of dealing with poverty. Perhaps more importantly, how actions *must* follow any declarations. "This conference confirmed that the way in which the church followed its own exhortation would largely determine whether its people would listen to it. Action must accompany new commitments."[27] Archbishop Oscar Romero, reflecting years later on the documents produced at Medellín, spoke about the episcopal conference's conversion to the needs of the poor: "[Conversion] is only possible through *accompanimiento*, when the church as the people of God accompanies its most vulnerable members in their lives and with their burdens."[28]

The bishops of Latin America and the Caribbean met again at Puebla, Mexico, in 1979. The concluding document affirmed the preferential option for the poor, a central theme of the Medellín conference and *Populorum Progressio*. Puebla was also impacted by *Evangelii Nuntiandi*. "Puebla discusses concretely the various challenges to evangelizing the culture today (*Puebla*, 420–423). Yet none of this is intended to negate the strong affirmations of the Medellín conference in favor of liberation and social justice."[29] As Bergoglio later reflected on these emerging themes, his own theological evolution was maturing. "Bergoglio continues to steer an independent path, with his characteristic passion for justice and love of the poor. This puts him on course to assume a major role of leadership in the Latin American Church by the end of the century."[30]

A clear focus of Puebla was the manifestations of faith in the culture of the people. "The popular religiosity that has developed over the centuries is no superficial cultural appendage but rather a depository of profound values that provide wisdom to the people in their historical sojourn."[31] Bergoglio knew that the people of Latin America looked at their faith through the lens of cultural traditions. The option for the poor, the dominant theme of Medellín, was supplemented in his thinking by the cultural tradition of the people. Puebla had been a huge breakthrough. "It now became possible to look at Latin America through its own cultural tradition, preserved above all in the spiritual and religious resources of the ordinary faithful people rather than through the lens of imported or elite ideologies."[32]

The document produced by the CELAM Conference in Aparecida, Brazil (2007), reverberates throughout *The Joy of the Gospel*. Jorge Bergoglio was a prime architect of the text. It was also influential in providing a *process*—the model used for episcopal synods in Rome by Francis. "Rather than working from a predetermined document, it began with a diagnosis of contemporary culture and trends from each country, then worked them into concrete issues that could be discussed. It was bottom-up, not as in the synods, top-down."[33] The document strongly encouraged a new approach to evangelization. "Aparecida was the expression of a new maturity of a local Church come of age....In its vision and vigor, its fierce advocacy of the poor and its missionary spirituality, its bold proclamation of the birth of a new springtime of faith, Aparecida was now the program, the key to a major new effort of evangelization in Latin America."[34] Bergoglio and the bishops at Aparecida spoke of the poor as *sobrantes*—the "left-over" people, extraneous to a market economy. They were the *cultura del descarte*, "the throw-away culture: the poor, the elderly, the children, the migrants—these were now dispensed with like out-of-date gadgets."[35] Aparecida is written in the theology of the *pueblo fiel*, the faith of the people. "As a result, Aparecida could safely unleash, to a greater extent even than Medellín in 1968, the riches of the Latin American Church, and give flesh to its great insight, the option for the poor, which appears dozens of times."[36]

The Aparecida document, with its attention to the faith of the people, concern for the poor, and the call to missionary discipleship, is an integral message of *The Joy of the Gospel*.

This apostolic exhortation, with its hope for the Church, did not instantaneously burst forth. It was the culmination of Jorge Bergoglio's life: his Jesuit training, his leadership positions within the Jesuit community, including provincial superior, service as auxiliary bishop and archbishop in Argentina, a member of the College of Cardinals, and his leadership role in the Church in Latin America and its episcopal conference. A strong influence on Bergoglio and his vision is the Second Vatican Council. Not to be discounted, perhaps most influential in creating the "joy of the gospel" in Jorge Bergoglio were familial and other friendships and associations that influenced his personal formation and shaped his sensitivity to the poor and marginalized.

FOR REFLECTION AND DISCUSSION

1. Of the many experiences that impacted Pope Francis's vision for *The Joy of the Gospel*, which seems most influential? Why? What has been most influential in your own development as a follower of Jesus Christ?

2. One important part of Jorge Bergoglio's theological development was the *pueblo fiel*, the theology of the people, a bottom-up theology that was derived from the teachings of the Second Vatican Council. How is this theology best utilized in a practical way in the Church today? In the diocese? In the parish?

3. It has been observed that good leaders have a healthy sense of themselves "flaws and all" and can work collaboratively. Why is integrity and personal commitment necessary for pastoral leadership?

4. In serving as a pastoral leader, what was the quality considered most important to Bergoglio? Why? How would you describe his pastoral style? How did this impact his pastoral priorities?

5. What are some of the contributions made to ecclesiology, of *being Church*, made by the bishops of Latin America and the Caribbean in their post–Vatican II documents? How did these documents, especially the document issued at Aparecida, influence the content of *The Joy of the Gospel*?

6. Pope Francis gives great import to Pope Paul VI's apostolic exhortation *Evangelii Nuntiandi*, On Evangelization in the Modern World. Its key premise is summarized in its statement, "Modern man listens more willingly to witnesses than to teachers and if he does listen to teachers, it is because they are witnesses." How can this principle best be utilized in the mission-oriented thrust of the parish promoted in *The Joy of the Gospel*?

7. The document produced by the Latin American and the Caribbean bishops at Aparecida, built on the theology of the people (*pueblo fiel*), is infused with concern for the *sobrantes*, the "left-over" people, those seen as extraneous in the market economy. This theme pervades *The Joy of the Gospel*. How can this concern be manifested and implemented in our missionary discipleship?

Chapter 2

THE ENCOUNTER

The joy of the Gospel fills the hearts and lives of all who encounter Jesus.

Evangelii Gaudium 1

The Joy of the Gospel insists on the overhaul of the way we do church. Such a dramatic transformation demands the conversion of mind and heart born of an encounter with Jesus Christ. We can never be the same again.

Missionary discipleship embarks on a journey not with an institution but with *a person*. It forces us to leave the path of least resistance and instead commence the journey with the essential. When Jesus sent his first disciples on mission, he dispatched them without much equipment: no carry-on bag or water bottles. They were not to call ahead for reservations. They would accept the hospitality from the people in whose homes they stayed. Their most indispensable asset was Jesus and what he had taught them. They were mesmerized by the Teacher and Prophet, and they too were compelled to change the world. "Thanks solely to this encounter—or renewed encounter—with God's love, which blossoms into an enriching friendship, we are liberated from our narrowness and self-absorption. We become fully human when we become more than human, when we let God bring us beyond ourselves in order to attain the fullest truth of our being" (*EG* 8). The dynamism of the commitment comes from only one thing: Jesus—his personality, personal authority, teaching, and relationship to his Father. So total was this attachment that the first disciples could give up everything—even their lives, if required.

> The Lord does not disappoint those who take this risk; whenever we take a step toward Jesus, we come to realize that he is already there, waiting for us with open arms. Now is the time to say to Jesus: "Lord, I have let myself be deceived; in a thousand ways I have shunned your love, yet here I am once more, to renew my covenant with you. I need you. Save me once again, Lord, take me once more into your redeeming embrace." (*EG* 3)

So too must this conversion be the impetus for the Church. "Here we find the source and inspiration for all our efforts at evangelization. For if we have received the love which restores meaning to our lives, *how can we fail to share that love with others?*" (*EG* 8, emphasis added). The Church is more than administration and rules. It is now urgent, Pope Francis declares, to see its role in a new way. "Each Christian and every community must discern the path that the Lord points out, but all of us are asked to obey his call *to go forth from our own comfort zone* in order to reach all the 'peripheries' in need of the light of the Gospel" (*EG* 20, emphasis added). Overwhelmed by the encounter with Jesus, the Christian, walking with the Church, wants to share Jesus as *the* companion for the journey. After their own encounter, the missionary disciple goes forth to say, like the first disciples, "I have found what I have been searching for!"

Pope Francis also realizes that most Christians have heard the Gospel stories for so long that it is hard to separate them from institutional trappings such as dogma, doctrine, and moral teachings that can delay or cloud the personal encounter with Jesus. So, he begins *The Joy of the Gospel* with an invitation to an encounter or renewed personal encounter with Jesus Christ.

Speaking to the bishops at Aparecida, Pope Benedict noted, "The first invitation that Jesus makes to every person who has lived an encounter with Him, is to be His disciple, so as to follow in his footsteps and to be a part of His community."[1] The first invitation extended by Jesus to the searcher is to become a disciple. As Andrew and John follow Jesus along the Sea of Galilee they ask Jesus where he lives. He responds, "Come and see." Something charismatic and overpowering in Jesus immediately attracts. The dynamic begins: the disciple wants more people to know this Jesus. This is missionary discipleship: bidding another to taste the sweetness of an encounter and to grasp serenity. "Being a Christian is not the result of an ethical choice or a lofty idea, but the encounter with an event, a person, which gives life a new horizon and a decisive direction."[2] The encounter happens. A decision must be made. Jesus is the answer. Will we allow Jesus to change our life? If we accede to the allurement, our lifestyle will go in a new way—the Way of the kingdom of God. The follower looks at the Master's standards and appropriates them. Everything else now seems superficial or distracting. Jesus becomes the *only* Way. It is Jesus's good news and not one's own. There are no other options. Everything is Jesus.

What does Jesus give us? What do we have to lose in letting Christ into our lives? "We lose nothing, nothing, absolutely nothing of what makes life free, beautiful and great. No!" declares Pope Benedict. "Only in this friendship are the doors of life opened wide. Only in this friendship do we experience beauty and liberation....Do not be afraid of Christ" (*Aparecida* 15).

Could making Jesus Christ a priority be an escape to an emotionalism or an abandonment of authentic spiritual and/or psychological struggle? "Anyone who excludes God from his or her horizons falsifies the notion of 'reality' and in consequence, can only end up in blind alleys or with recipes for destruction" (*Aparecida* 15). It is not escaping reality to embrace this friendship. "Only in this friendship is the great potential of human existence truly revealed" (*Aparecida* 15).

The God we know is a God with a human face. A God who will go to the cross for us. When the disciple appreciates the depth of this friendship, he cannot but respond with love, "I will follow you wherever you go" (Luke 9:57).

Embracing the gift of friendship with Jesus is the joy of the gospel. Feasting on the Word of God must be our steady diet, since the words of Jesus are "spirit and life" (John 6:63). The disciples, formed as servants of the Word, propose Jesus's friendship to their brothers and sisters. The Eucharist confirms the disciple in evangelization and a strong desire to preach the gospel to form a more just society. "From the Eucharist, in the course of the centuries, an immense wealth of charity has sprung forth in the difficulties of others, of love and of justice."[3] The Eucharist is not solely for my own nourishment; it feeds me so that I may feed others. The Eucharist cannot be separated from the love of neighbor.

"Love of God and love of neighbor have become one; in the least of the brethren we find Jesus himself, and in Jesus we find God."[4] Jesus comes to bolster relations between people. As St. John Chrysostom warned, "Do you wish to honor the Body of Christ? Do not ignore him when he is naked. Do not pay him homage in the temple clad in silk, only then to neglect him outside where he is cold and ill clad."[5] The Eucharist is the radiating center of life in Christ and the unbreakable bond between the love of God and the love of neighbor inviting all to "overcome grave social inequalities and the enormous differences in access to goods."[6] The encounter with Jesus moves us to service. We embrace the kingdom teachings of Jesus in the beatitudes, knowing that, like Jesus, commitment to these precepts leads us also to embrace the cross, in integrity and courage. "Let us not be afraid of the cross, intrinsic to the faithful following of Jesus, because it is illuminated by the light of the resurrection" (*Aparecida* 2). The disciple, gazing at the face of Jesus in his suffering and ultimate victory over death, sees through the eyes of faith the humiliated faces of many people yearning to be respected for their human dignity as daughters and sons of God.

People today hunger and thirst for the life and happiness that can only be provided by Christ. Many hunger and thirst for a new life, formed in God's Word and refreshed by the Bread that comes down from heaven. After an encounter with Jesus, we crave to manifest the joy of being a disciple. "We want the joy that we have received in the encounter with Jesus Christ whom we recognize as the Son of God incarnate and redeemer, to reach all men and women wounded by adversities; we want the good news of the Kingdom of God, of Jesus Christ, victorious over sin and death, to reach all who lie along the roadside, asking for alms and compassion (cf. Luke 10:29–37; 18:25–43)" (*Aparecida* 29). It is a joy that is "not a feeling of selfish well-being, but a certainty that springs from faith, that soothes the heart, and provides the ability to proclaim the good news of God's love" (*Aparecida* 29). Knowledge of Jesus is the best gift that can be offered and the best gift that can be received. In him we are renewed: "In communion with [Christ] we hope to find life, the true life that is worthy of the name, and thus we want to make him known to others, to communicate to them what we have found in him" (*Aparecida* 3).

The disciple grows in awareness that he or she is beloved of God and redeemed in Jesus Christ, the risen one, who frees from all slavery, to live in justice and fraternity. "*Discipleship* and *mission* are like the two sides of a single coin: when the disciple is in love with Christ, he cannot stop proclaiming to the world that only in him do we find salvation (cf. Acts 4:12). In effect the disciple knows that without Christ there is no light, no hope, no love, no future" (*Aparecida* 3). In Jesus, we are free and alive. "Jesus is the way that allows us to discover the truth and to achieve the total fulfillment of our life" (*Aparecida* 1). Such an embrace of Jesus Christ helps us to avoid entwining faith only with dogmatic truths: "a Catholic faith reduced to mere baggage, to a collection of rules and prohibitions, to fragmented devotional practices, to selective and partial adherence to the truths of the faith, to occasional participation in the sacraments, to the repetition of doctrinal principles, to bland or nervous moralizing that does not convert the life of the baptized, would not withstand the trials of time" (*Aparecida* 12). The bishops warned of a trend that had been identified by then Cardinal Joseph Ratzinger: "Our greatest danger is the gray pragmatism of the daily life of the church in which everything apparently continues normally, but in reality the faith is being consumed and falling into meanness."[7] We herald that only life in Christ heals and humanizes. Discipleship develops in the hearts of those in whom the impact of encountering Jesus has been transformative. "While we suffer and rejoice, we remain in the love of Christ viewing our world, we try to discern its paths with the joyful hope and indescribable gratitude of believing in Jesus Christ" (*Aparecida* 21).

Missionary discipleship, according to Pope Francis and *The Joy of the Gospel*, begins with an encounter with Jesus. This experience of being embraced by Jesus, Son of God, the Savior, who comes to share our burdens and impart God's peace and friendship begins the believer's journey. The disciple commits to building the kingdom, nourished by Word and Sacrament—going out to the peripheries and sharing the good news that Jesus has come to set us free.

FOR REFLECTION AND DISCUSSION

1. The missionary discipleship outlined by Pope Francis in *The Joy of the Gospel* builds on the relationship with Jesus Christ and not on an institutional approach. Why, according to Pope Francis, is it necessary to begin discipleship with the person of Jesus? How does an individual enhance that relationship or even begin that relationship when lacking? How does a faith community?

2. What do the New Testament Scriptures identify as illustrations of the commitment of the first disciples

to follow Jesus? How is Jesus challenging our personal sense of commitment to discipleship? Our faith community's commitment?

3. It is difficult to serve others, especially the poor and the marginalized, if we have not experienced how God first loved us. Why is this experience essential to a solid commitment to discipleship?

4. As we reflect on the New Testament, it seems clear that there was an immediate attraction by the first disciples to Jesus. What is the dynamic that flows from the encounter with Jesus that results in undertaking the commitment to discipleship?

5. St. John Chrysostom warned, "Do you wish to honor the Body of Christ? Do not ignore him when he is naked. Do not pay him homage in the temple clad in silk, only then to neglect him outside where he is cold and ill clad." What is the intrinsic relationship between our worship of God and the need to be of service to those in need?

6. When Pope Benedict met with the bishops of Latin America and the Caribbean at Aparecida, he stated, "From the Eucharist, in the course of the centuries, an immense wealth of charity has sprung forth in the difficulties of others, of love and of justice." How can we assure that the Jesus Christ we consume at the Eucharist is also shared with the wider community?

Chapter 3

PARISH LEADERSHIP

When we adopt a pastoral goal and a missionary style,
which would actually reach everyone without exception
or exclusion, the message has to concentrate on the
essentials, on what is most beautiful, most grand, most
appealing, and at the same time most necessary.

Evangelii Gaudium 35

According to *The Joy of the Gospel*, there is a comforting joy that
comes from evangelizing. "Goodness always tends to spread. Every
authentic experience of truth and goodness seeks by its very nature
to grow within us, and any person who has experienced a profound
liberation becomes more sensitive to the needs of others" (*EG* 9).
There is an opportunity to live life "on a higher plane," when one
embraces a life that gives itself away. "When the Church summons
Christians to take up the task of evangelization, she is simply pointing
to the source of authentic personal fulfillment" (*EG* 10).

God constantly challenges those who believe "to go forth." The
Scriptures are replete with examples of God's call to set out in mission,
including Abraham, Moses, and Jeremiah who was told, "You shall go
to all to whom I send you" (Jer 1:7). Each person and each community
discerns a direction for the missionary journey in response to Jesus's
command to "go and make disciples." We are all summoned to set off

for the peripheries wherever they might be, but with one constant: "to go forth from our own comfort zone" (*EG* 20).

The missionary option is the key to the transformation of the Church "so that the Church's customs, ways of doing things, times and schedules, language and structures can be suitably channeled for the evangelization of today's world rather than for her self-preservation" (*EG* 27).

The Joy of the Gospel affirms the value of the parish—the place "where the hungry come to be feed and the thirsty come to drink." To be effective, it is necessary that the parish (or any ecclesial structure) have a flexibility for missionary discipleship. The genius of the parish, the pope points out, is its potential and adaptability. "The parish is not an outdated institution; precisely because it possesses great flexibility, it can assume quite different contours depending on the openness and missionary creativity of the pastor and the community" (*EG* 28). The parish mission takes shape as formed by many variables, including location. A parish that is situated in a struggling, economically challenged neighborhood can have a different orientation for mission than a parish that is located in a middle-class or above middle-class neighborhood. It will also be significantly impacted by available resources, both in personnel and finances. The contours of parish ministry can vary greatly, influenced especially by the creativity of its leadership. Is the leadership capable of imagining opportunities for service and new approaches for guiding such service? Is there familiarity with the appropriate technology that could direct the missionary commitment? Are there new parishioners or parishioners of long-standing with talents yet to be employed that can be tapped?

The parish is established canonically with designated territorial boundaries. But a map of a parish with its streets and avenues cannot render the flavor of a neighborhood, fully reproduce the cultural identity, or become alive "in the homes of her sons and daughters" (*EG* 28).

A key starting point for mission engagement is a careful analysis of the demographics of race, age, and economic status of the parish territory Before embarking on a pastoral plan, our cathedral staff and parish council combed through data provided by the diocese from a contracted service provider. The statistical material, based on the current U.S. census and multiple other data feeds, identified the following:

- A stable but diverse population (total population of 18,140 with 1 percent decline since 2010); 7,053 households;
- Black and Hispanic communities were experiencing the fastest growth. The average household income was $48,869, with over 20 percent of households making $15,000 or less; 35 percent or more were living in poverty;
- Most people were "working poor";
- Due to a significant, recent influx of refugees in the area, the Asian presence had swelled to 10 percent of the total population;
- Approximately one-third of those in our neighborhoods identified as Roman Catholic.

The data graphically demonstrated a transformation of needs. What was once a blue-collar and middle-class neighborhood had morphed gradually into a community that was deep in poverty with its consequent effects: high unemployment, lack of adequate food and housing, rife with abusive relationships and single-parent households. The challenges for revitalized missionary discipleship were daunting.

The Joy of the Gospel characterizes the parish as an *environment for hearing God's word*. The Scriptures are prayed over and acted upon. God's word is our living memory of the events of our salvation history. "The joy of evangelizing always arises from grateful remembrance: it is a grace which we constantly need to implore" (*EG* 13). As the parish explored potential initiatives, the leadership attuned itself to God's word. What would God have us do? What was the word of God speaking to our hearts? Attentive to the proclamation of God's word at the table of the Lord, the community was prepared to ask God, What would you have us do?

A primary responsibility of parish leadership is to engage the entire parish in mission. "The important thing is to not walk alone, but to rely on each other" (*EG* 33). The community encounters the Lord at his table, through the sacraments, and in prayer. It is tempting to remain on the mountain in the glow and comfort of Jesus's glory (Matt 17:1–8). But Jesus comes down from the mountain and turns his eyes toward Jerusalem. So, too, the disciple leaves what is comfortable and goes into the world. "A missionary heart...never closes itself off, never retreats into its own security, never opts for rigidity and defensiveness...it always does what good it can, even if in the process, its shoes get soiled by the mud of the street" (*EG* 45).

Pope Francis encourages parish leadership to be creative while using *The Joy of the Gospel*, adapting it to circumstances. But it should be followed with courage. "I encourage everyone to apply the guidelines found in this document generously and courageously, without inhibitions or fear. The important thing is to not walk alone, but to rely on each other as brothers and sisters, and especially under the leadership of the bishops, in a wise and realistic pastoral discernment" (*EG* 33).

In leading the parish in mission, Pope Francis spends time describing what pastoral leaders should *not* do:

TEMPTATIONS FACED BY PASTORAL WORKERS (*EG* 76–101)

The Challenge of Missionary Discipleship

Pastoral ministers can be absorbed in the quest for personal freedom, which shows itself in a variety of circumstances. We tend to see missionary discipleship as an "add-on" to already established routines. We can be reluctant to collaborate with other staff or parishioners—our carefully prepared plans will be compromised when others "interfere" with recommendations that veer from the original plan. It takes humility to be willing to listen, reflect, and possibly change our opinion.

The pope warns of segregating ministry opportunities to times, circumstances, and situations when it is convenient and comfortable. He also advises ministers to be alert to negative self-consciousness, fed by doubts about the effectiveness of one's pastoral ministry. "Many pastoral workers, although they pray, develop a sort of inferiority complex which leads them to relativize or conceal their Christian identity and convictions" (*EG* 79). The demands can be overwhelming. "[Pastoral ministers] end up being unhappy with who they are and what they do; they do not identify with their mission of evangelization and this weakens their commitment" (*EG* 79). This lack of coherence with the mission leads to a profound disconnect. "This practical relativism consists in acting as if God did not exist, making decisions as if the poor did not exist, setting goals as if others did not exist, working as if people who have not received the Gospel did not exist" (*EG* 80). Clearly, those infected will be severely alienated from the joy of the gospel. "It is striking that even some who clearly have solid doctrinal and spiritual convictions frequently fall into a lifestyle which leads to an attachment to financial security, or to a desire for power or human glory at all cost, rather than giving their lives to others in mission" (*EG* 80).

No to Selfishness and Spiritual Sloth

It is a temptation to limit opportunities for service, with the assertion that personal time is necessary. "This [limitation in time to ministry] is frequently due to the fact that people feel an overbearing need to guard their personal freedom, as though the task of evangelization was a dangerous poison rather than a joyful response to God's love which summons us to mission and makes us fulfilled and productive" (*EG* 81). With the demands today, the amount of time given in ministry can be extraordinary and overwhelming. Pastoral ministers must take time for personal renewal, days off, and vacations. It can be tempting to arrange one's ministry around time away that becomes the default. *The Joy of the Gospel* wonders if the problem here may not be *activity* but rather *motivation*—or lack thereof. *Accedia* (spiritual apathy) can develop from multiple causes: unrealistic expectations, unwillingness to have patience for projects to mature; an obsession with obtaining immediate results; a loss of contact with people that so depersonalizes one's work that we "are more concerned with the road map than with the journey itself" (*EG* 82). A "tomb psychology" can develop—being caught up in darkness and weariness. "Let us not," says the pope, "allow ourselves to be robbed of the joy of evangelization!"

No to a Sterile Pessimism

Pope John XXIII, at the beginning of the Second Vatican Council, sensing pessimism regarding the great undertaking about to take place, warned against "prophets of doom." Pope Francis also admonishes about a serious temptation of pastoral workers: defeatism—giving up before we even start. We give up, forgetting the words of Jesus to St. Paul: "My grace is sufficient for you, for power is made perfect in weakness" (2 Cor 12:9). The pope warns against a "spiritual desertification" that can occur in the family or in the workplace when it becomes parched and lifeless, where the roots of faith need to be revitalized. Yet it is also in the desert that many find what is essential for living. "And in the desert people are needed who, by the example of their own lives, point out the way of the Promised Land and keep hope alive. In these situations, we are called to be living sources of water from which others can drink" (*EG* 86). We cannot, the pope contends, allow ourselves to be robbed of hope.

No to Spiritual Worldliness

The temptation of "spiritual worldliness" arises from hearts centered on the rewards of human glory and personal well-being. It is cultivated in careful appearances, and outer appearances are usually much easier to judge than what comes forth from the heart. We are tempted to have a feeling of superiority that comes from compliance with rules and certain disciplines that can lead to a "narcissistic and authoritarian elitism"—conducive to analysis and classification of others, but not to evangelization. This spiritual worldliness leads to seeing the life of the Church "as a museum piece or something which is the property of a select few" (*EG* 95). It orients our assessments to the observable in evaluating parish life: a business mentality or management by statistics, focusing on the institutional Church but not the people of God. "The mark of Christ, incarnate, crucified and risen, is not present; closed and elite groups are formed, and no effort is made to go forth and seek out those who are distant or the immense multitudes who thirst for Christ. Evangelical fervor is replaced by the empty pleasure of complacency and self-indulgence" (*EG* 95). This danger must be avoided at all costs, declares the pope, by the Church always looking outwardly, to the peripheries, "keeping her mission focused on Jesus Christ, and her commitment to the poor" (*EG* 97). The cure is inhaling the "breath of the Holy Spirit," which frees us from self-centeredness and merely external outward religiosity. "Let us not allow ourselves to be robbed of the Gospel!" (*EG* 97).

No to Warring among Ourselves

The struggle of spiritual worldliness identified above as an obsession with outward appearances, can lead to a battle mentality within the parish and within the Church. The lines are drawn easily and quickly with a turfdom approach to mission. There always seems to be much at stake. Our priorities easily reveal our ecclesiology. At Sacred Heart, our cathedral staff and consultative bodies have identified the needs of the poor, especially in our own neighborhood, as having precedence. Some parishioners ask that the priorities of the parish (including budget resources) focus on a more comprehensive, doctrinal lifelong faith formation. They are not mutually exclusive goals. There is always the risk of "camps" with competitive interests coagulating into inflexible positions. "Some are even no longer content to live as part of the greater Church community but stoke a spirit of exclusivity, creating an 'inner circle.' Instead of belonging to the whole Church, in all its rich variety, they belong to this or that group which thinks itself different or special" (*EG* 98). *The Joy of the Gospel* asks, "How many wars take place within the people of God *and in our different communities!*" (*EG* 98, emphasis added).

The pope's antidote is to love one another "in spite of everything....We all have our likes and dislikes, and perhaps at this very moment we are angry with someone....To pray for a person with whom I am irritated is a beautiful step forward in love, and an act of evangelization" (*EG* 101). He adds a warning: "Beware of the temptation of jealousy! We are all in the same boat and headed to the same port! Let us ask for the grace to rejoice in the gifts of each, which belong to all" (*EG* 99).

Yes to the New Relationships Brought by Christ

To say yes to Christ is to say yes to relationships. The joy from the gospel is solidarity and encounter. "To go out of ourselves and to join others is healthy for us. To be self-centered is to taste the bitter poison of immanence and humanity will be worse for every selfish choice we make" (*EG* 87). The temptation in pastoral life is to become attached to our needs and our vision, so much so that we escape to our ruminations, removed from the social gospel and its demands. It is easy to rely on computer screens for our satisfaction and the immediate sense of control they offer. The gospel calls for face-to-face encounters with people, their pain and joys, which can be life-giving for us as well. "True faith in the incarnate Son of God is inseparable from self-giving, from membership in the community, from service, from reconciliation with others. The Son of God, by becoming flesh, summoned us to the revolution of tenderness" (*EG* 88). Much of Francis's pontificate has centered on "accompaniment," of walking along with others in their journey. It is the mode and style suggested by *The Joy of the Gospel* and a cure for an overly self-centered approach to ministry. "We need to help others to realize that the only way to learn how to encounter others with the right attitude, which is to accept and esteem them as companions along the way, without interior resistance. Better yet, it means learning to find Jesus in the faces of others, in their voices, in their pleas" (*EG* 91). Here we find true healing, in a fraternal love capable of finding God in every human being and in seeking the happiness of others.

Ordained ministers struggle to know how they best serve and the exact nature of their role within the community. The lay members of the Church struggle as well—and continuously ask questions about their function in the ministry that they rightfully believe they are called to. Pope Francis calls the Church to *synodality*, a walking together, with members acknowledged, appreciated, and listened to. With the diminishing of ordained ministers in the Church, it is urgent that lay members be entrusted with more responsibilities as baptized members of the Christian faithful. This is particularly urgent regarding the role of women in service to the Church. "But we need to create still broader opportunities for a more incisive female presence in the Church" (*EG* 103). Our own cathedral community has been greatly enriched, as have many parishes, by the selfless commitment of women who can accompany others in their journeys in ways that men cannot.

"Challenges exist to be overcome! Let us be realists, but without losing our joy, our boldness, and our hope-filled commitment" (*EG* 109).

FOR REFLECTION
AND DISCUSSION

1. Pope Francis speaks to a "comforting joy" that comes from evangelizing. What are the dynamics of missionary discipleship as taught in this apostolic exhortation that lead to the joy of the gospel?

2. Although each person and community must discern a direction for the missionary journey, what, according to Pope Francis, is the one constant? How does this constant affect a faith community's willingness to undertake missionary discipleship? What efforts can be taken to overcome any initial resistance?

3. *The Joy of the Gospel* affirms the importance of the parish, "where the hungry come to be fed and the thirsty come to drink." In what ways should this description be applicable to the parish? What are some ways that a parish or any faith community could satisfy the hunger and thirst of those who approach for nourishment?

4. What are the variables that affect the contours of missionary discipleship undertaken by a parish? What is the most important variable that sets direction for ministry? What might be the negative variables that counteract the possibility of missionary discipleship?

5. Are designated territorial boundaries established to limit parishes? Why is it important to analyze the demographic data of a parish before developing missionary strategy? What are the most important demographics of a parish that shape a pastoral plan?

6. The pope warns against the segregating of ministry opportunities to when it is convenient and comfortable. What might be ways to overcome a general or a more specific malaise that interrupts, delays, or even prevents evangelization?

7. *The Joy of the Gospel* notes the challenge of "spiritual desertification" present at times in the family, at the workplace, and even in the Church, when faith becomes parched and lifeless and needs revitalizing. What tools might be effective in bringing about a needed reenergizing?

Chapter 4

THE PEOPLE OF GOD

> If something should rightly disturb us and trouble our
> consciences, it is the fact that so many of our brothers
> and sisters are living without the strength, light and
> consolation born of friendship with Jesus Christ,
> without a community of faith to support them.

Evangelii Gaudium 49

The Joy of the Gospel is emphatic that the entire people of God
participates in the mission of the Church. It speaks of an evangelizing
community of missionary disciples "who take the first steps, who are
involved and supportive, who bear fruit and rejoice" (*EG* 24). This
participation of all God's people was a major theme of the Second
Vatican Council: "It has pleased God, however, to make men
holy and save them not merely as individuals without any mutual
bonds, but by making them into a single people, a people which
acknowledges Him in truth and serves him in holiness" (*Lumen
Gentium* 9).[1] Pope Paul VI, in *Evangelii Nuntiandi*, also reiterated
the task of all God's people in missionary outreach: "But who then
has the mission of evangelizing?...it is upon the Church that 'there
rests, by divine mandate, the duty of going out into the whole world
and preaching the gospel to every creature'" (*Declaration on Religious
Liberty*, 13). In another text: "The whole Church is missionary,
and the work of evangelization is a basic duty of the People of God

(*Ad Gentes* 35)" (*Evangelii Nuntiandi* 59).[2] Over the centuries, the Church had emphasized a clerical approach to ministry built on the sacramental role of the ordained within the community. The task of evangelizing was also entrusted to their care as teachers of the faith. They could be assisted by others such as women religious and catechists who had been trained for this role. In the ecclesiology that developed, particularly from the Council of Trent and until the Second Vatican Council, the laity were viewed principally as receivers of the sacraments and of the teachings of the Church. They had little participation in the governance of the institution and passively functioned. The passivity was perhaps best illustrated by the lack of active participation in the celebration of Mass. Although the Second Vatican Council highlighted the sacrament of holy orders in two specific decrees on the episcopacy and presbyterate, the importance of the sacraments of baptism and confirmation was also emphasized.

> Incorporated into the church by Baptism, the faithful are appointed by their baptismal character to Christian religious worship; reborn as sons and daughters of God, they must profess publicly the faith they have received from God through the church. By the sacrament of Confirmation, they are more perfectly bound to the church and are endowed with the special strength of the holy Spirit. Hence, as true witnesses of Christ, they are more strictly obliged both to spread and to defend the faith by word and deed. (*Lumen Gentium* 11)

Gradually and incrementally, the laity have become more engaged in the mission of the Church. The laity became increasingly active in parish life with the development of parish pastoral councils, where parishioners joined their pastors to plan and execute pastoral strategies for the parish. To assist bishops and pastors in their accountability for the patrimony of the diocese and parish, diocesan and parish finance councils were instituted. They would advise bishops and pastors in areas related to the proper stewardship of parish funds and their administration, areas not necessarily within the domain of expertise of the typical bishop or pastor.

Developments such as these promoted the importance of the sacraments of baptism and confirmation, allowing the members of the Catholic community in every parish to become involved and personally invested in the mission of the Church.

In the Aparecida document, there is a strong focus on the role of the laity, as disciples and missionaries of Jesus Christ, Light of the World. The people of God must live out their commitment to be disciples by an active, lived expression of their baptismal commitment.

> We call on the Holy Spirit in order to be able to provide a profound witness entailing close affection, listening, humility, solidarity, compassion, dialogue, reconciliation, commitment to social justice, and ability to share, as Jesus did. [The Holy Spirit] keeps calling, keeps inviting, keeps offering constantly a worthy and full life for all…this means setting out from our isolated minds and throwing ourselves with courage and confidence [*parrhesia*] into the mission of the entire Church. (*Aparecida* 363)

The laity are bolstered for their outreach to the peripheries by confirmation.

The Joy of the Gospel explains, "An evangelizing community knows that the Lord has taken the initiative, he has loved us first (cf. 1 John 4:19), and therefore we can move forward, boldly take the initiative, go out to others, seek those who have fallen away, stand at the crossroads and welcome the outcast" (*EG* 24). The incentive comes from an interior renewal, intensified by an experience of Jesus Christ that demands a response—to share with others what one has received by grace. The pattern takes place in all God's people: to gaze at Jesus, to be transformed, to gaze at the world—our neighborhoods, our cities, our areas—and then to proclaim the good things that the Lord has done.

A few years ago, our parish, like many, faced a serious financial challenge, an upcoming fiscal year with a severe budget deficit. When meeting with the bishop and his staff to discuss the impending deficit, it became obvious that fixed items—heat, electricity, building maintenance, and the like—could not be significantly reduced. Because we had a large campus, with a school building, former convent, rectory, and worship space, and since the school and convent provided needed rental income, the only option for significantly decreasing the deficit was cutting staff. At the time, we had a full-time pastoral associate, a music director, a director of social ministry, parish secretary, finance director, bookkeeper, faith formation director, and maintenance personnel. The finance personnel were shared with three other city parishes. The pastoral staff was employed full-time for the parish. The only viable, but very difficult choice, was to either eliminate or reduce to part-time the pastoral staff. Recognizing the need to maintain the mission of the parish (why maintain buildings if they are not used for ministry?), we reduced the pastoral staff to part-time.

After reflection and much discussion, we formulated an approach to ministry that we hoped would not only maintain our mission but also enhance it. We gathered with several key parishioners actively engaged in the life of the parish, including members of the parish and finance councils, social ministry, and so on, and discussed a proposal that would need their support. Our parish had developed missionary outreach to the poor, migrants, and neighborhood children. The staff shared how the parish had embraced and generously supported these initiatives. The pastoral staff also recognized that they would not be serving the parish forever and that it was important that the parish assume more responsibility for these ministries and embracing the parish mission. We shared our idea about identifying members of the community who would serve as "parish ministers." We held an orientation session for twelve parishioners who seemed well suited.

They met with our staff for three sessions of discernment so they could ask questions, discuss, and pray about whether they had the time and desire for this opportunity. Ultimately, nine agreed to enter formation for this new ministry.

The candidates would work with an individual staff member for a joint development of the ministry that would be undertaken along with regular supervisory sessions. Ongoing theological education would be provided to all the parish ministers by the staff and a retired scripture professor from a local college who had volunteered to help coordinate the program. We also invited some outside resource people with certain specializations, including spiritual life development. These formation opportunities would take place once a month over several months, usually following the last Sunday morning Mass. The sessions were informal, lasting approximately an hour and a half, consisting of a presentation and dialogue. The content included reflection on Pope Francis's vision of ministry, the use of Scripture in the spiritual life, a demographic study of the parish with a focus on the diversity of the population of the parish, the importance of liturgy to the parish community, and the role of women in the Church. The material was integrated into the practical issues of ministry. The parish ministers identified the area of ministry and the staff member they would work with. One parish minister, a choir member, would work with the parish music director, assisting with the practical details of scheduling rehearsals and various logistics that were a part of organizing the cathedral choir. Another two parish ministers were assigned to work with the cathedral pastoral associate, whose ministry included coordinating the parish liturgical ministries. The two parish ministers assisted in scheduling liturgical ministers, while another parish minister accepted the training program for new liturgical ministry volunteers as well as the renewal program for veterans. Both parish ministers accepted these responsibilities with enthusiasm, and the pastoral associate now devoted more energy to other areas of ministry greatly needed due to the reduction in paid hours.

Two other parish ministers worked with me in our outreach to the homebound elderly, hospital, nursing homes, and senior facilities. Like most parishes today, the age of the cathedral population skewed older. The parishioners in these facilities remained vitally important to the parish, and we reinforced the connection with visits by a parish minister. Identification badges were prepared for them, and they completed the appropriate diocesan training for contact with the vulnerable.

One weekend, they alternated speaking at the end of each Mass, explaining their ministry and outreach to the homebound and senior facilities, and made themselves available in the church's lobby after Mass for any parishioners who might have names of family members or others who might appreciate a visit. Some names were submitted, but, surprisingly, several parishioners volunteered to visit shut-ins and nursing homes. It was an overwhelming affirmation of the community's concern for the many who could not be physically present and the desire to make sure that these parishioners did not feel excluded or abandoned.

The coronavirus pandemic was the occasion for a mobilization by these parish ministers to enlist more members of the parish to keep contact with the sick and homebound. Many responded and the ministry became an even more effective means for outreach.

Two parish ministers asked if they could work with the cathedral's social ministry coordinator. This coordinator's responsibility included oversight of the various outreach ministries, including Joseph's Place, the parish food pantry. As the number of people from the neighborhood using the pantry grew, the complexities multiplied: finding food to stock the shelves, volunteers to assist, maintaining procedures for orderly and safe distribution, and so on. Other ministries associated with the pantry were also begun (see chapter 5).

At the same time, the social ministry coordinator was involved in myriad neighborhood outreach efforts including an annual summer hot dog roast sponsored by the parish. Free hot dogs, chips, and sodas were available in the parish parking lot, along with games for children, information booths staffed by police and firefighters, and programs directed by various health organizations. An annual heritage festival brought neighbors to the cathedral to join in a special Sunday Mass celebrating our gift of rich diversity, followed by a colorful procession in the neighborhood with many parishioners in native costumes. Everyone then gathered in the cathedral hall for a great banquet featuring various native dishes from a variety of countries, including Myanmar, Bhutan, Vietnam, and the Congo.

Our social ministry coordinator, working with the social ministry committee, inaugurated "community dinners." Every quarter, meals were prepared and guests from Joseph's Place and the neighborhood were invited to break bread with our parish family. Many parishioners were involved in preparation, serving, and cleanup. It became a welcome opportunity for the parishioners who worshipped regularly at the church to meet their neighbors, many of whom appreciated not only the hospitality but also the opportunity to tour the cathedral church that many had often passed by but had been reluctant to enter. Information was provided about the worship opportunities at the cathedral and services available from the parish.

Due to the extent and intensity of the social outreach of the parish, our social ministry coordinator was stretched for time. He very much appreciated the assistance of parish ministers who could assist in the administration of the outreach ministries.

It was important that the parish ministers be identified and accepted by the entire parish. An insert was distributed through the parish bulletin providing the rationale for the ministry, with a picture and brief biography of each of those who had accepted this new role. The parish ministers were installed at one of the weekend liturgies. A rite of commissioning was created. Each candidate was called forward after the pastor's homily and stood with the staff member they would be working with. The presider and the community prayed for empowerment by the Holy Spirit in their service to the parish. Each new parish minister received a badge with their name and the designation "Parish Minister."

At the conclusion of the rite, the assembly joined in sustained applause. After Mass, the newly installed parish ministers were congratulated and thanked at a social conducted in the church's lobby.

Clearly, in the future more ministries will be needed and led or supplemented by parish ministers. They will be identified by the community and leadership of the parish for a variety of opportunities for service. The charisms of the individual members of the community will be continually fostered and these people recruited. It will also be an opportunity for theological education, not only for the parish ministers, but also for the staff, councils, and committees. Offered regularly, this enrichment serves also as an important ingredient of the Christian journey—lifelong learning about Jesus and his message.

Pope Francis speaks often of "synodality"—a governance model for "being Church." In the early Church, bishops gathered to examine common problems, came to a consensus, and formulated a policy or law. Pope Paul VI revived synodality during the Second Vatican Council in an effort toward more collegial governance. A synod of bishops would be convened regularly to study issues of importance for the universal Church. Several synods have been held in intervening years on a variety of topics, most recently on the challenges to the Church in the Amazon region. Unfortunately, the synodal assemblies became listless, recycling solutions that had been tried—and failed—before. Pope Francis appealed to the synods to be bolder and more creative, with honest and respectful dialogue, honoring new approaches and ideas that emerge from honest conversation.

So, too, the parish can use the synodal model. Fresh approaches and novel ways of walking and working together as a parish can enhance its vitality. As a pastor, I often find that an honest conversation with the parish council members gives me fresh insights. It is a reminder that we are in this together. Synodality respects the input of the community, honors the integrity of the one from whom the observation emerges, and focuses on the mission, often in creative ways. Such discussions result in new ministries and a strengthening of our mission. They help us overcome the temptation of "being shut up, within structures that give us a false sense of security, within rules which make us harsh judges, within habits which make us feel safe, while at our door people are starving" (*EG* 49). Most importantly, they keep the people of God involved.

FOR REFLECTION AND DISCUSSION

1. What is the appropriate impact of the sacraments of baptism and confirmation on the role of the laity in the Church today? How can that role best be exercised? Are there opportunities for the distinct charisms of the laity to be utilized that are presently undeveloped in the parish and other faith communities?

2. Parish pastoral councils have presented the local Church with opportunities for the sharing with the parish gifts and expertise that can help with pastoral planning. How would you assess from personal experience the participation of the people of God in the mission of pastoral planning for the parish? What is needed to better utilize the gifts of the members of the people of God?

3. Finance councils were mandated by the 1983 Code of Canon Law to assist pastors in the proper stewardship of financial resources and temporalities. What are the unique contributions of both pastors and the laity that serve on parish finance councils to financial accountability?

4. How does a pastoral staff best discern the gifts that are needed to best serve a parish community and the means to best call forward from the congregation those gifts?

5. The Aparecida document that is frequently referenced in *The Joy of the Gospel* speaks of the Holy Spirit who

"keeps calling, keeps inviting, keeps offering a constantly a worthy and full life for all." How can parish leadership move its members from an isolation to a more confident participation in missionary discipleship?

6. One possibility for utilizing the baptismal gifts and charisms of the members of a parish community is by designation of specific members for committed service and providing proper theological, pastoral training. Are there opportunities present that would make this an effective addition for missionary discipleship?

7. How is the model of designated parish ministers from the community best incorporated into the life of the entire parish?

Chapter 5

TO THE PERIPHERIES

I prefer a Church which is bruised, hurting and dirty
because it has been out on the streets, rather than a
Church which is unhealthy from being confined and
from clinging to its own security.

Evangelii Gaudium 49

The Joy of the Gospel insists that our pastoral ministry cannot be
limited to an "obsession with a disjointed transmission of a multitude
of doctrines to be insistently imposed" (*EG* 35). Rather, the pastoral
goal is "to actually reach everyone without exception or exclusion...
to concentrate on the essentials, on what is most beautiful, most
grand, most appealing, and at the same time, most necessary" (*EG*
35). It is the transmission of a *relationship* with Jesus, which the
missionary disciple has experienced, and the fostering of this love
for Jesus in others. The emphasis is on *relationships*—one's personal
experience with Jesus. The pope demands that the Church refrain
from a self-referential bias, of being too inwardly focused. Instead,
it must be outer directed—to the peripheries, to places not within
the normal field of vision of the community, which always results
from self-absorption. *The Joy of the Gospel* imagines a Church that is
bruised, hurting, and dirty, which only materializes if we go beyond
self-imposed boundaries and to the margins. Nourished and sustained
by the Eucharist, the followers of Jesus must also become "feeders"

after being fed. "You give them something to eat," says Jesus when surrounded by so many who hunger and thirst, whom he does not wish to send away. This command is given to all of us. We must look beyond our own needs and see the many who hunger and thirst for basic life necessities and who search for some reason why they suffer. It is unhealthy, avers *The Joy of the Gospel,* to be confined by our own needs, clinging to what is secure. We cannot do ministry as we have always done it. "I invite everyone to be bold and creative in this task of rethinking" (*EG* 33). Novel approaches push us outward toward places and people we need to see with the gaze of faith.

Pope Francis visualizes the role of the Church as a "field hospital," akin to a medical unit in a war zone treating the wounded and dying. "I see clearly...that the thing the church needs most today is the ability to heal wounds and to warm the hearts of the faithful; it needs nearness, proximity."[1] The initial diagnosis is crucial. You don't treat a serious arm wound by medicating the patient for high cholesterol. We can't prescribe for a headache when the patient is bleeding. The cure must match the wound. The Church must offer a medicine of the heart to the many who come to her with interior pain. As we discussed earlier, inner loneliness is not healed solely by social media platforms.

Many come to the Church traumatized. A field hospital can be a very messy place.[2] It lacks all the usual refined instruments and medical resources that are part of a modern-day hospital. The medical personnel in a field hospital often must make do. They use what they have in the most effective way. Lacking equipment and sufficient personnel, teamwork is essential. They bring skills and history to their work.

The parish should also operate as a field hospital, available to the various outcasts and the marginalized, often doing treatment without all the needed resources, yet with the most important spiritual resources: deep faith and a missionary mandate. Parishes are called to struggle with maladies both physical (such as a need for food, clothing, housing, or employment) or interior (the hunger for love, better family relationships, issues of self-esteem). With limited resources, the parish must fully utilize resources of the parish community, carefully integrating the talents of the members in response to the needs. There may be physicians, attorneys, or financial advisors, as well as some adept in spiritual counseling, scriptural, theological, and liturgical studies, and other disciplines that can address crises in the community that cry out for healing. In issues of social justice, the healing often requires strong advocacy, so that the sepsis of discrimination, segregation, and stereotyping can be purged.

Several years ago, our parish unearthed an obvious population in need on the peripheries of our neighborhood. Two parishioners had discussed over coffee the increasing number of refugees in our area. They were particularly disturbed by the number in the neighborhood walking streets in the cold Rochester winter wearing sandals and not shoes. They wondered what the parish could do for them. With research, they learned that the Catholic Family Center, an affiliate of Catholic Charities in the Diocese of Rochester, worked with arriving refugees, providing initial financial support and American inculturation. This inculturation was time-restricted, due to the large number of refugees constantly arriving. After three months, the refugee was basically "on his [her] own," as the understaffed and underfunded agency shifted its resources to the latest arrivals. These parishioners identified a need by recognizing the refugees' precarious transition and the resource gap. Concerned parishioners gathered to discuss the challenge. More data was provided by parish staff members who had attended a briefing by the local city government on the essential needs of the burgeoning refugee population. A plan was formulated by this new team. The recently vacated rectory of a nearby church would be the outreach center and would collect food and clothing for the refugee families.

The needs expanded, and so too did the services required. Included on the site of the new refugee outreach were a church building, a school building, and a convent. The property was sold to a nonprofit housing corporation that converted the campus to affordable housing. The church building would be rented back to the cathedral as a new home for "Mary's Place." After renovations, including the erection of large room dividers, partitioning for classes and activities, the former worship space was now the center for expanded ministries that could serve the refugees, many of whom resided in the neighborhood. In addition to food and clothing, it now offered English-language tutoring, assistance in applying for green cards for permanent residency status, citizenship, and caseworker aid for the personal and family challenges, as well as employment assistance. When local retail merchants discovered that the refugees were industrious and dependable, several were hired. Many had arrived from refugee camps (the average stay was seventeen years) and were frugal and careful in the management of their personal finances. An independent nonprofit was established to buy and rehab homes in the area to offer affordable housing. As professional service needs for the refugee community expanded, Mary's Place became its own 501c nonprofit, with the cathedral maintaining representation on the board of directors.

Mary's Place is a vital outreach ministry for those making traumatic adjustments to a new way of life. It has been the beneficiary of many grants and is recognized as a vital link to the needs of an important segment of the community. Many of the Karenni, a Sino-Tibetan ethnic group native to the Kayah State of Myanmar (Burma) are Catholic and worship together at one of the weekend cathedral Masses. A highlight for our community was the baptism of twenty-five Karenni, adults and children, celebrated by a native priest visiting from Myanmar. Once a month, a Karenni parishioner proclaims the first Scripture reading at Mass in Kayah, with an English translation provided on our worship aid card.

In the 1970s, the cathedral parish joined with neighboring churches to begin a joint effort at feeding the poor in the neighborhood. It was called M.E.E.K., the Maplewood Edgerton Emergency [K]upboard and was an initiative that fostered an ecumenical spirit, uniting several neighboring faith communities with a united mission:

feeding the poor. Food collected by the various church communities would be stored and distributed once a week from one of the local Protestant churches. A few years ago, it became evident that more and more people were coming to the cathedral for food. It also became evident that feeding the hungry was becoming a more urgent problem. The ministry of M.E.E.K. needed to be augmented by our own parish initiative. At a parish pastoral council meeting a member suggested that the parish take up a food collection once a month at Mass, requesting certain items that could be gathered in bulk—a "Food Frenzy Weekend." The parish responded enthusiastically, and a hefty amount of food was collected. Where should we distribute the foodstuffs? Many options were debated, including M.E.E.K. However, as an increasing number of families in the neighborhood were turning up at the cathedral for food, it was obvious that a food pantry should be located at the cathedral itself. Because M.E.E.K. was open for four days a week except Wednesdays, the new food pantry at the cathedral would be open on Wednesdays.

Because the parish had established a ministry to refugees called "Mary's Place" (one of the founders of the ministry had great devotion to the mother of Jesus), the pantry would be called "Joseph's Place" for the spouse of Mary and as a tribute to the Sisters of St. Joseph who had taught at the cathedral school for many years and continued to serve the parish in a variety of pastoral ministries after the school was closed. The new ministry would be housed in a wing of the convent where the sisters had resided for many years.

A team of parishioners designed a vision for the operation of the pantry. Everyone who came would be treated as a guest. Bags of food would not be simply handed to the guests. A "food minister" would sit with each guest in a waiting area to record basic information about their family and other needs besides food. Although Joseph's Place did not have the capacity to satisfy every need, an up-to-date resource manual was available. Each guest would be directed to adjoining rooms stocked with food and other supplies. The individual, assisted by the food minister, would select the products most needed. There were restrictions placed on the number of items from the categories (canned vegetables, soups, etc.) so that product availability could be maintained for those who would come later. Seventeen guests came to the door at Joseph's Place on March 25, 2015. More and more families came, and the ministry has likewise expanded. In the summer of 2015, "Joseph's Garden" was planted in the former parochial school playground adjacent to the pantry, where fresh fruits and vegetables were grown. Duties for gardening and harvesting were shared equally among Joseph's Place ministers and guests who volunteered. The food produced was brought to the Joseph's Place pantry shelves, much to the satisfaction of the guest gardeners who delighted to participate in feeding others, making them more than just recipients of food distributed.

In April 2016, "Joseph's Attic" was established and located in an unused bay of the rectory garage. "Slightly used" furniture was donated by parishioners that volunteers would pick up and later deliver to neighborhood homes. There was a rapid turnover in the many apartments and duplexes in the neighborhood, so furniture was always in demand.

When it first launched, Joseph's Place was open for service two days a month. But as the need for food became more and more urgent, starting in July 2016 it would be open an additional day for food.

Carefully assessing needs from the guests' input, Joseph's Place began a collaboration with Rochester Works to provide job training programs and skills.

In March 2017, Joseph's Place celebrated its second anniversary. It was now serving over seven hundred families annually and had provided over sixty-two thousand meals since its opening. In May 2017, Joseph's Garden began an "Adopt-A-Crop" program, inviting parishioners and guests to donate extra fruits and vegetables grown in their gardens to Joseph's Place.

In March 2018, Joseph's Place celebrated its third anniversary and had served over one thousand families and had provided food for more than 125,000 meals. By March 2019, it had served over twelve hundred families in the area. When a nonprofit agency that had rented space in the former convent where the pantry was also housed decided to relocate, Joseph's Place decided to expand into the formerly occupied space. More shelving could be accommodated as well as more freezer space. More rooms could be designated for individual counseling and shared prayer, ensuring more privacy. It seemed also an appropriate opportunity to expand services, such as basic medical screenings, including checks for blood pressure, weight, and pulse rate. To augment other employment initiatives, providing tutoring in preparation for high school equivalency exams was explored.

A vital spiritual foundation for the work at Joseph's Place was highlighted. Ministers participated in a day of recollection to reflect on the mission: the call of Jesus to be present to the poor, the vulnerable, those in need, and to feed them as mandated by Jesus in Matthew 25. The pantry was never to become a mere social service. It was to be strongly motivated by the compassion of Jesus Christ and service in his name. The ministers gather for prayer before the pantry doors are opened, to seek God's grace for their service. They also pray for the many benefactors who contribute financial resources for the food and other supplies that are needed. They live the "accompaniment" spoken of by Pope Francis: They "remove their sandals before the sacred ground of the other" (cf. Exod 3:5), making present "the fragrance of Christ's closeness and his personal gaze" (*EG* 169). This accompaniment develops the art of listening, sensitive to the sorrows of a fellow pilgrim—their guest. "The peace of this accompaniment must be steady and reassuring, reflecting our closeness and our compassionate gaze which also heals, liberates and encourages growth in the Christian life" (*EG* 169). The Joseph's Place Mission Statement guides its efforts: "To welcome and honor the 'hidden Christ'; treat each person with dignity and respect; assume only the best of intentions."

Joseph's Place and Mary's Place are efforts to travel to the peripheries in discipleship, to leave what is comfortable and to be where we are needed. It is the response to Jesus: "You give them something to eat." It flows naturally and automatically from gathering in the eucharistic assembly: to be fed at the table of the Lord and then to go and feed others, especially those on the periphery. Pedro Arupe, a former Jesuit Superior General has said, "The Eucharist is not complete when there are still people in the world who hunger." No matter how many people are fed, there will still be more who need to be fed. Although we cannot feed everyone, it is a start—one person at a time.

FOR REFLECTION AND DISCUSSION

1. According to *The Joy of the Gospel,* what is the pastoral goal of pastoral ministry? What should remain the focus of all pastoral initiatives?
2. The pope expresses concern that at times the Church has a "self-referential bias," being too inwardly focused instead of more outer directed. Where is that outer direction best focused?
3. The pope uses the image of a "field hospital" for how the Church should operate in today's world. Is this an appropriate image for a parish and its mission? How best can a faith community tend to the variety of circumstances of pain that inflicts so many? What is the best "medicine of heart" that the Church can use to alleviate inner pain?
4. How can advocacy by a community best assist in healing for those issues that impact social justice?
5. Are there initiatives operative in your own faith community that seek to respond to immediate needs for food, clothing, and shelter? What could be the first-actions step that could guide the community in making a response to a serious need?

6. In *The Joy of the Gospel*, Pope Francis states his desire for a Church that is "bruised, hurting and dirty." Why is this vision, according to the pope, so necessary for missionary discipleship?

7. Pope Francis frequently mentions the "peripheries," those areas and populations of the marginalized of society, whose presence and needs are often ignored. How can this population best be acknowledged and integrated into the faith community?

Chapter 6

THE POOR

Just as the commandment "Thou shall not kill" sets a
clear limit in order to safeguard the value of human life,
today we also have to say "thou shall not" to an economy
of exclusion and inequality. Such an economy kills.

Evangelii Gaudium 53

In *The Joy of the Gospel*, the pope is adamant about the need to go to
the peripheries, especially to serve the poor. As William Werpehowski
describes it, the concern expressed by Pope Francis builds solidly on
a tradition of Catholic social justice.[1] It is not surprising that this
pope would be particularly concerned about the poor, given his own
personal experience. His family was not well-off. He witnessed the
dichotomy between the rich and the poor in his native country of
Argentina. His roots as a Jesuit exposed him to the concern of this
religious congregation for the poor. As a bishop, he was familiar with
the magisterium that had characterized the bishops of Latin America
and the Caribbean in the documents from Medellín and Pueblo. He
had been the facilitator at the 2007 conference held at Aparecida,
which continued the tradition of these conferences in speaking truth
to power—to those responsible for the inequality that was pervasive.
As the archbishop of Buenos Aires, he sent priests to the poorest
sections of the archdiocese. Clearly, concern and service to the poor
was an important moral priority for him.

POPE FRANCIS AND THE PARISH

The Joy of the Gospel treats extensively an imperative: The Church must be docile to the cries of the poor, avoid a self-centered pragmatism, and listen to the needs of those in need. The pope's Jesuit tradition emphasizes meditation, prayer, and the interior life, as found in the spiritual exercises of St. Ignatius. But he also recognizes the necessary connection between the spiritual life and the summons to go out to the peripheries. Love of neighbor links the "fixed tabernacle" with the "mobile tabernacles." Celebrating the Eucharist and service to the poor cannot be separated.

Service to the poor cannot be compromised or slowed by a need to have outreach ministries fully developed and operational before venturing out to serve. Pope Francis warns of an "efficiency-ism"—thinking that the Church is all right if she has everything under control, if she lives without shocks, with the agenda always in order, all regulated. Jesus doesn't send a carefully crafted agenda and organized plan; rather, he sends the Holy Spirit to guide the effort.

Data does have its place. In Rochester, New York, a major study was published about the pervasive poverty that afflicted the area: "Poverty and the Concentration of Poverty in the Nine-County Greater Rochester Area."[2] The report identified Rochester as the second poorest among comparably sized cities in the United States. It is the fifth poorest city in the country among the seventy-five largest metro areas. It has the third largest concentration of extremely poor neighborhoods and the poorest school district in Upstate New York; 19 percent of children in the nine-county area are poor. In the city of Rochester, nearly half of the children (46 percent) are poor. The contrasts by race is startling. The poverty rate stands at 34 percent of the population for Blacks, 33 percent for Hispanics, and 10 percent for Caucasians. Blacks and Hispanics had a much higher rate of poverty in the city of Rochester than they do elsewhere in New York State or even in the nation.

There was a strong public reaction when the report was issued. Blame was generously distributed as to the whys. The editorial pages of the local newspaper were filled day after day with angry letters, often generating more heat than light. Pastors resolutely preached about the inequality that must be addressed. It could no longer be "business as usual" in the community.

One positive initiative with promise was the Rochester-Monroe County Anti-Poverty Initiative (RMAPI), a multidisciplinary task force with state funding that brought together community leaders with different areas of expertise. The effort was charged with the task of reducing poverty by 50 percent over the next fifteen years. Several task forces were created: "Build and Support Community," "Address Structural Racism," and "Address Trauma." An executive director was hired to manage and organize the processes. Reports to the community have been issued regularly, and some victories have been achieved. There has been a slight diminution of the poverty level, but it remains difficult to gauge the level of racism and bias. Even with the reduction of poverty, statistical evidence cannot show whether the presence of racism has decreased.

The Church's role remains urgent: feeding the hungry, giving drink to the thirsty, clothing the naked, and sheltering the homeless, but just as important is the advocacy that addresses the structural bias that has caused the poverty. Pope Francis identifies the role the Church must play: "If we want to bring about deep change, we need to realize that certain mindsets really do influence our behavior. Our efforts at education will be inadequate and ineffectual unless we strive to promote a new way of thinking about human beings, life, society and our relationship with nature" (*Laudato Si'* 215).[3]

The Joy of the Gospel specifically addresses the needs of an urban culture, where poverty is often extreme. Pope Francis instructs us to look at the city with a contemplative gaze, a "gaze of faith which sees God dwelling in their homes, in their streets and squares" (*EG* 71). We often look at our cities warily, with fear. The problems are massive: unemployment, squalid living conditions, and educational disparities. Francis asks us to gaze with Jesus's eyes: "God's presence accompanies the sincere efforts of individuals and groups to find encouragement and meaning in their lives. He dwells among them, fostering solidarity, fraternity, and the desire for goodness, truth and justice" (*EG* 71). Jesus's gaze, when he looked at the people of his time, saw their potential as followers but also recognized impediments preventing them from fully embracing his message. He knew humanity and did not need anyone to explain it to him (see John 2:25). Jesus knew the lifestyle of an urban context, yet he gazed with compassion, providing grace and the experience of God's love. When we look at the city with a contemplative gaze, we view a common humanity, filled with a broad mosaic of "different lifestyles and different rhythms" that is *alive*, not at "non-citizens, "half-citizens," or "urban remnants." The pope is a realist: "In many parts of the world, cities are the scene of mass protests where thousands of people call for freedom, a voice in public life, justice and a variety of other demands which, if not properly understood, will not be silenced by force" (*EG* 74). There are countless possibilities and opportunities. "Jesus desires to pour out an abundance of life upon our cities" (*EG* 75). It is the "unified and complete sense of human life that the Gospel proposes that is the best remedy for the ills of our cities. It is the Gospel that will be the leaven, the Gospel witness in every city that will make us better Christians and help us to bear fruit" (*EG* 75).

When the cathedral community expanded the physical facilities of Joseph's Place, the food pantry, it also realized that it was urgent to expand other programs as well. *The Joy of the Gospel* identifies several needs of the poor. "We are not simply talking about ensuring nourishment or a 'dignified sustenance' for all people, but also their 'general temporal welfare and prosperity.' This means education, access to health care and above all, employment, for it is through free, creative, participatory mutually supportive labor that human beings express and enhance the dignity of their lives" (*EG* 192). Joseph's Place began exploring tutoring for those in need of help in obtaining high school equivalency. Conversations were held with agencies who provided related information and materials. A confidential survey was conducted with the guests who frequented Joseph's Place to find out if this might be a need. Several indicated that they would definitely appreciate the opportunity for tutoring for the high school equivalency exam. Planning is currently underway to assess the logistics.

Many of the guests who come to Joseph's Place have struggled with various addictions. Thankfully, a suburban-based addiction recovery program has made information and assistance available to the guests of Joseph's Place.

Some of the guests who come to Joseph's Place also have served prison time. Conversations with our guests have indicated that many have had a member of their family who has served time or is presently serving time. This has led to a search for a Christian response to incarceration. In 1990 the U.S. bishops issued *Responsibility, Rehabilitation and Restoration: A Catholic Perspective on Crime and Criminal Justice*, a comprehensive approach to criminal justice reform. Drawing on theology and scripture, the document reflects on our Christian tradition of justice—and mercy. In his visit to the United States in 2015, Pope Francis included in his itinerary a visit to the Curran-Fromhold Correctional Facility in Philadelphia. He has also washed the feet of prisoners during the Holy Thursday Mass of the Lord's Supper.

So we asked ourselves, How can we best assist those who are seeking a road to recovery and restoration in society? How do we best minister to those who have lost a loved one to violence? One recommendation in the bishops' document is "restorative justice," where an opportunity is given to the perpetrator of a crime to reflect with others on the impact of his actions on the victim and on the community. The victim can participate in the process. The role that parishes have in supporting the families of the incarcerated is also emphasized, especially children who have lost a parent to prison time.

The parish is invited to become aware of the multiple ethical questions in criminal justice, including the death penalty, bail reform, and solitary confinement. It is also important to assist the victims of crime who need support ministry. These efforts can involve networking with other parishes and state Catholic conferences for systemic change, such as no longer using punishment as a deterrent. Usually, punishment such as prison time is administered as retribution. Without an opportunity for reform, the risk of recidivism remains high. The parish can be helpful in creating a community that seeks to prevent opportunities for crime, especially among the young. When a person convicted of a crime leaves prison, they are provided few resources for the adjustment to a free life. They often return to the lifestyle that led them to incarceration: using and selling drugs, larceny, and so on. Working collaboratively with other churches and organizations, a parish can provide resources that assist transition, key to preventing recidivism.

Our parish began its work of "visiting the imprisoned" by simply inviting parishioners to write a Christmas card to Christian inmates at the local jail. An announcement was made about the opportunity, and tables were set up in the church's lobby with cards and mailing labels with a prisoner's name and address. Immediately after Mass, with the assistance of a parish prison ministry team, many parishioners sat down to write a personal note on the cards provided. The signed cards were collected and mailed with postage supplied by the local Knights of Columbus. The deacon, who is a chaplain at the jail, shared the effect of this effort. Many inmates expressed their gratitude for these cards, and some shared that it was the only Christmas card they received. Remarkably, the number of inmates attending Mass increased. This simple act of sending an incarcerated person a Christmas card with a personal message of hope gave strength and consolation. So successful was this initiative that it was decided that it would continue at Easter, the celebration of new life and hope. Prayer booklets were also included in the mailing. This again garnered positive feedback and gratitude from the prisoners and chaplain staff.

The prison ministry team continues to explore new opportunities for "visiting the imprisoned," developing advocacy opportunities that can address the systemic challenges of criminal justice reform. It begins with a steady, contemplative gaze.

FOR REFLECTION AND DISCUSSION

1. Why is Pope Francis's concern in addressing poverty so personal? How did poverty affect his ministry in the Jesuit community and his experience as a bishop?
2. What actions taken by the pope when he was archbishop of Buenos Aires demonstrate his moral priority for outreach to the poor?
3. Pope Francis has spoken about the "fixed tabernacle" and the "mobile tabernacles." What does he see as the vital connection between the Eucharist and serving the poor?
4. What is the danger of waiting for statistical data and studies before beginning outreach to the poor? How can the accumulation of data in a particular area help in establishing a mission of outreach?
5. What is the role of advocacy in performing the corporal works of mercy?
6. The pope asks us to look at our cities with a contemplative gaze. How are we assisted in this vision when the problems and challenges of cities seem so massive and daunting today?
7. Many residents of cities, primarily members of a minority racial group, are often incarcerated or have served time in prison. How can the gospel declaration by Jesus—"When I was in prison you visited me"—become a part of a parish's missionary discipleship? How can this outreach become a part of advocacy for criminal justice reform?

Chapter 7

THE FOUR ESSENTIAL PRINCIPLES

> Progress in building a people of peace, justice and
> fraternity depends on four principles related to constant
> tensions present in every social reality.
>
> *Evangelii Gaudium* 221

In *The Joy of the Gospel*, Pope Francis directs attention to four essential
attitudes/principles to bring about the kingdom of God, "building a
people of peace, justice and fraternity":

1. Time is greater than space.
2. Unity prevails over conflict.
3. Realities are more important than ideas.
4. The whole is greater than the part.

TIME IS GREATER THAN SPACE

"Time is greater than space" means seeing and committing to following a course of action without being obsessed with results. "It helps
us patiently to endure difficult and adverse situations, or inevitable
changes in our plans" (*EG* 223). It can be a temptation in pastoral life

to focus on a strategy or goal, failing to see how often in the working toward that goal the ideas are seen as more important than achieving the goal. The team that planned the food pantry established a project with a dream—a day when the doors to the pantry would be opened, with people from the neighborhood appearing in considerable numbers to receive the food items that had been meticulously sorted and shelved. They dreamed about how the tables would be set up, the role of the ministers, and the process of distribution. Many meetings moved the project along, but there were many helpful insights that surfaced in their planning process, not only about the dynamics of the team—their interactions and working together—but also how this planning was impacting the entire parish community. As the team began to work on the project, they began to appreciate the individual talents of each member. One was a dreamer who envisioned the end product in vivid detail. Another was an organizer, able to visualize each step to arrive at the goal of the project efficiently. This team member identified in detail the possible pitfalls that could slow or even stop the progress. Another member of the team was a questioner, who analyzed each step and saw possible risks as well as the advantages of another direction. Another was an "encourager," keeping the team going when doubts arose. The encourager kept the team focused on the original reason for the ministry and how the food pantry would be consistent with the mission of the parish and the mission of the Church.

The parish community itself also changed as the project continued. As they learned of the progress, the parishioners became committed to the purpose of the project in terms of the mission. Parish committees now looked at their own work as part of a greater whole, an essential part of the mission of the parish. While the focus remained on the opening of the pantry, there was much discussion of the poverty in the neighborhood that had generated the initial goal. The "food frenzy"—the collection of food items after each Mass—became even more significant with more and more contributions. The collection of food and its destination developed a dynamic of its own. Families began to shop for their groceries with this in mind: "Don't forget to pick up extra for the food frenzy this weekend." Almost every family came to church with boxes and bags of donated food for the bins designated to receive them. A different member of the parish who had volunteered to work at Joseph's Place was present at every Mass, standing near the collecting station to thank the individuals and families who donated food. At each Mass, parishioners were invited to join the offertory procession of bread and wine, carrying a representative basket of food items, a gift for the poor. The food collection became in itself a part of building a pantry and building a community. If people forgot to bring food, they often donated money for Joseph's Place in the offertory collection so we would be able to purchase needed supplies. A "Friends of Joseph's Place" society was formed for members of the parish and friends who desired to make regular financial contributions to support the pantry and who would be apprised by a newsletter of the work being done.

The parish had a goal: to create a food pantry to feed the hungry, especially people of the neighborhood. Early on, the team that worked directly on the project realized that some of the detours on the way enhanced rather than hindered its success. It was remarkable to see how in committing to an action and not obsessing over the results led us to a food pantry that brought along the way so many unimagined blessings.

UNITY PREVAILS OVER CONFLICT

There is always a tendency, when a team studies an issue and formulates an action plan, for differences of opinion to stall or even stop the work. "Conflict cannot be ignored or concealed. It has to be faced. But if we remain trapped in conflict, we lose our perspective, our horizons shrink and reality itself begins to fall apart. In the midst conflict, we lose our sense of the profound unity of reality" (*EG* 226). Several years ago, when the growing population of the refugee community became obvious, it was clear that some action was necessary. Two options surfaced. Catholic Family Center, a part of Catholic Charities operating in the Diocese of Rochester, had been working on the resettlement of the refugee population for several years. Over time, they had amassed the necessary resources to help the new arrivals. Should the refugee population in our neighborhood be handed over to Catholic Family Center and their expertise? Others argued that this was a unique opportunity for the parish itself to respond to Jesus: "I was a stranger and you welcomed me."

A consensus emerged: The parish would create its own program to assist the refugees in the neighborhood. As it studied the issues related to the arrival of refugees, it came to know more about the approach of Catholic Charities. Their work was principally in assisting the new arrivals with their initial orientation by initiating tutoring in the English language, orienting them to a new lifestyle and culture—understanding the mysteries of shopping at a supermarket, using currency, acclimating to public transportation—and conducting a preliminary orientation for job-skill training. The program, however, was limited to three months, necessitated by the logistics: the number of refugees and the staff available from Catholic Family Center to provide the needed services. "Mary's Place," the new cathedral refugee ministry, would attempt to take up where Catholic Family Center left off. After providing winter clothing, volunteers from the parish would provide English-language instruction. Using the former rectory of a nearby parish, classes began. The parish recognized the need as immediate.

Hundreds of refugee families have been assisted by the work of Mary's Place. Although the number of refugees admitted to the United States and subsequently to Catholic Family Center and Mary's Place diminished due to federal immigration policy, the ministry continues to reach and welcome a sizable number of families. Mary's Place has also grown along with the refugee population, networking with numerous other agencies. Through successful fundraising efforts, the ministry has been vitalized and expanded. A fruitful series of conversations—not always concluding with unanimity about a course of action, but united in a commitment to serving our neighbors in need—has brought about a thriving ministry that continues to serve many, consensus prevailing over conflict.

REALITIES ARE MORE IMPORTANT THAN IDEAS

It is often a temptation for parish leadership to spend an enormous amount of time talking about the challenges of poverty, unemployment, migrant and refugee ministry, criminal justice, life issues, and so on. There is a danger that these challenges can be relegated to the realm of ideas. "Realities simply are, whereas ideas are worked out" (*EG* 231). Flowcharts and diagrams are assembled and statistics are analyzed—sometimes *ad nauseam*. Pope Francis says, see not "issues" but "people." We can look at the information provided by data as both the problem and the solution. A diocesan representative once came to our parish and gave a presentation to the parish council with statistical data about our community, including the number of households, the predominant religious affiliations, the range of ages, the level of income, the number of single-parent households, and so on. The data seemed overwhelming. Addressed as well were needs including more daycare facilities and more crime prevention for personal safety. What could possibly be done with our limited resources to assist a community with so many problems? We were tempted to thank the speaker and move on to the next item on the agenda. The data was undeniable, but the facts were more than data. It was reality and lived experience, human faces with needs. Many parishioners live outside the official boundaries, but many had lived in the city and for a variety of reasons, including the changing demographics of the neighborhood, had moved to the surrounding suburbs. Some returned to the cathedral for weekend liturgies and, as they drove in and out, could see the dramatic changes that had taken place. We now had the opportunity to invest time and resources into what we often *looked at* but did not always *see*. With the gaze of contemplation, it was clear that action was needed. It was urgent that we go to the peripheries, right outside our doors, with refugee outreach, food pantry, community dinners, wellness center, job training, and high school equivalency help. Ideas cannot remain just ideas; they must become reality.

THE WHOLE IS GREATER THAN THE PART

One function of a pastoral team and other parish leadership is to orchestrate the various "parts"—the individual ministries and pastoral initiatives—as well as manage financial resources into a cohesive whole. In 2016 our parish pastoral council and staff began work on a strategic five-year plan. We asked ourselves the following: Where would we like to see ourselves in five years? And what would we need to do to get there? One member of the parish council had extensive experience in strategic planning and kindly offered to guide us in the journey. We first needed to revise our parish mission statement. That would help us to know where we were going. The consensus was that a new, more vital statement was imperative. The ministry needs of the parish were evolving and so must a mission statement that gives some direction. It was also the consensus that a parish mission statement requires the support and endorsement of the entire parish. The parishioners would personally absorb it and assess their present and future participation. Every council, committee, and organization would use this statement as its lodestar, united by their faith in the gospel of Jesus Christ, committed to walking together in mission.

A draft of the mission statement came to the parish council for prayer, reflection, and consensus. Although received with enthusiasm, especially for its focus on the cathedral as a "community of hope," bringing the good news to the poor, some tweaking was necessary. It was then enthusiastically endorsed. With the support of the parish staff, the mission statement was published in the parish bulletin and on the website, as we sought input from the parishioners at large. Review of the feedback revealed unambiguous parish support and affirmation of the new mission statement as the reference point for the parish in its planning venture.

The parish council conceived the course of action for the formulation of the five-year plan: a task force generated a comprehensive survey, and the team canvassed the parish consultative bodies, committees, and organizations. After the input was collected, the parish council and staff analyzed the data and classified the responses into predominant themes: liturgy, communication, social justice, and finances. A summary vision was attached to each category. We invited parishioners to join a task force for one of the themes, based on their experience and interest. Their charge was to develop concrete action steps and a five-year timeline for the theme. One Saturday, during a five-hour session, teams formulated a series of action steps for each theme. For example, under finances, the goal was an annual balanced budget. To achieve that, the parish would conduct a capital campaign that could stabilize the income by providing for needed, costly repairs for the aging buildings. After an endorsement by the parish council and staff, the five-year strategic plan was presented to the parish councils, committees, organizations, and the parish at large for study and endorsement.

This five-year plan equipped us with a unifying theme for all of our ministries. We were socially engaged in vital ministries, and we were a family that delighted in gathering each weekend for the Eucharist, with many members involved in liturgical ministries, participating in a variety of social events, and visiting the sick and the homebound. We were, like so many parishes, busy and active. The strategic five-year planning gave us a pause—a needed pause. We stopped, prayed, and reflected. With all we were doing, did we have a mission? Had we redoubled our efforts and lost track of the cause? We had to ask, Why do we do what we do? Was it because we had always done it, and it was what a parish should do? Because it had been mandated by the bishop or by canon law? How effective had we been as a community in communications? Did our ministry concentrate so exclusively on activities that we failed to address structural causes or deficiencies that precipitated need for outreach? *The whole is greater than the part* had provided our leadership with an important lens to move forward. "We constantly have to broaden our horizons and see the greater good which will benefit us all....We can work on a small scale, in our own neighborhood, with a larger perspective" (*EG* 235). We no longer saw each committee, council, or organization as an end in itself. Our parish mission statement was critical in setting the direction.

FOR REFLECTION AND DISCUSSION

1. One of the four essential principles described by Pope Francis in *The Joy of the Gospel* is that "time is greater than space," which enables us to "endure difficult and adverse situations, or inevitable changes in our plans." Are there advantages to approaching tasks related to ministry not being obsessed with results? Are there disadvantages?

2. Have you had experiences where, in working toward a goal, the process itself produced results as significant or more significant than achieving the goal?

3. In working toward an objective as a team, many important roles for the individual members often emerge: dreamer, organizer, questioner, encourager. How can each of the various roles be integrated into a working whole? Should one role be dominant?

4. Another principle is "unity prevails over conflict." What dynamics can best be utilized when a difference of opinion threatens to stall or even stop a project?

5. "Realities are more important than ideas." Analysis causing paralysis can deter strong action plans intended to address a gaping need. While acknowledging the importance of careful planning and the accumulation of appropriate data, how best can a parish avoid the pitfall of feeling overwhelmed by information to the extent that action is not taken?

6. When the pope refers to the principle "the whole is greater than the part" he discusses people getting "caught up in an abstract, globalized universe, falling into step behind everyone else, admiring the glitter of other people's world, gaping and applauding at all the right times" (*EG* 234). He describes another extreme in which people are "doomed to do the same things over and over, and incapable of being challenged by novelty or appreciating the beauty which God bestows beyond their borders." How do we balance both perspectives, seeing in our local community its native identity and beauty and, at the same time, the larger community and its contribution?

7. *The Joy of the Gospel* highlights how people, including the poor and their culture, their aspirations, and their potential, must be integrated into the whole of society. How is this made a reality in working for the common good?

Chapter 8

THE THREE-STEP PROGRAM

> But to live our human life to the fullest and to meet
> every challenge as a leaven of Gospel witness in every
> culture and in every city will make us better Christians
> and bear fruit in our cities.
>
> *Evangelii Gaudium* 75

There are many programs that are based on "steps." Perhaps the most notable is the "Twelve Steps" program of Alcoholics Anonymous. The progressive and essential steps provide guidance and support to the members. *The Joy of the Gospel* offers an implicit Three-Step Program, drawn from the Catholic social justice tradition and referenced in *Aparecida*, the CELAM document of 2007, edited by Pope Francis when he was serving as cardinal-archbishop of Buenos Aires.

SEE–JUDGE–ACT

The three steps of "see–judge–act" can integrate social justice with practical action. When applied to a parish, the first step is "to see," be *observant*. Social media, ubiquitous digital images, and data bombard us unremittingly. We are so absorbed in our own needs and our experiences of life that our perspective and range of vision is routine and limited. In *The Joy of the Gospel*, Pope Francis often speaks of a special *gaze*: to look at our cities with a contemplative gaze, a "gaze of faith"; "encountering the gaze of Jesus"; "the gaze of the Good Shepherd who seeks not to judge but to love"; "the gaze of tender love directed to Christ crucified"; "Christ's closeness and his personal gaze"; "our compassionate gaze which also heals, liberates and encourages growth in the Christian life"; "Jesus' gaze, burning with love, expands to embrace all his people"; and "a spiritual gaze born of deep faith which acknowledges what God is doing in the lives of others." "To gaze" is more than "to look at." It is to see with loving attention, reflection, and experience. To gaze at the city, according to Francis is *to see* with a contemplative gaze "God dwelling in homes," to see with the eyes of faith, to see struggles, death, poverty—and light.

As we carefully and intentionally examine the data of our experience, we can begin to ask ourselves what are the people in the situation doing, feeling, and saying? What is happening to them and how do they respond? How do I respond? How do we respond? We ask ourselves more specific questions:

- What do we know about the issue that is surfacing?
- Are there specific facts that I can identify about the issue(s) that surface from my observations?
- What am I learning as I continue to reflect?
- Does it touch me personally?

The next step is "to judge." This is not to make a moral assessment of a person's behavior, to determine who is in conformity with the mores of the society in which I live. For this process, it means analytics and investigation where our awareness of an injustice in our environment leads to an analysis. Who is affected? How are they being affected? Why are they being affected? The social sciences can be effectively utilized including sociology and psychology, which can provide data and research. We also use theological reflection, a dialogue with our religious tradition. How do Scripture and our Catholic social justice tradition interpret this experience?

A. Social Analysis[1]

Economic

- Are there ownership issues?
- Who are the actors involved?
- What are the economies and financial implications that are at work?
- Is someone or a group of individuals not receiving services who should?
- Are there implicit dynamics involved?

Political

- Who are the decision-makers and are there power differentials?
- Who is impacted by the decisions made?
- How are decisions made?
- Who are the decision-makers not involved?
- Why are they excluded?

Historical

- Is there a broader context from which the present situation emerges?
- Are there precedents or analogies that could be clarifying?
- Are there events from the past that have precipitated, influenced, or necessitated the situation?

Cultural

- Are there cultural values at stake? Are they imposed from the outside?
- Are there geographical and/or ethnical controversies that are a part of the dynamics?
- Are the cultural dynamics recent or historical?

B. Theological Reflection

There are several distinct but vital theological reference points that can underlie the theological analysis. Theological reference points include Scripture and the tradition of Catholic social justice.

Biblical

- Are there major themes in our biblical tradition that can interpret the experience?
- Can we identify biblical values that seem to apply to the issue at hand?
- What biblical themes seem pertinent?

Catholic Social Teaching

This tradition is often associated with Pope Leo XIII and his encyclical *Rerum novarum* (1891) on labor and management relationships. Many subsequent encyclicals by various popes continued to address matters of social justice: the dignity of the human person, family, community and participation, rights and responsibilities, option for the poor and vulnerable, the dignity of work and the rights of workers, solidarity, and care for God's creation.

- How does Catholic social justice and its principles apply to the situation?

The intense, steady observation of the environment, followed by the social and theological analysis, leads to the ultimate step, the most crucial: "to act."

- What can we do *now* to address immediate needs?
- What actions need to be taken to address the root cause, the systemic problem that has given rise to the situation?
- If no action can be taken at the present time, should more reflection, investigation, or research be undertaken?
- How could one empower those who seem to be disadvantaged in this situation?
- What can we do to *transform the structures* that have precipitated the injustice?

There should be a dose of reality about what actions may be effective. What are the skills of those who would assist in the action step(s)? Who and what other resources may be needed? It seems advisable to start small with a good plan, rather than to throw up hands with "there is nothing that can be done."

The "see–judge–act" approach, also has been described as "the pastoral cycle" and is associated with a Belgian priest, later cardinal, Joseph Cardijn, one of the fathers of the Second Vatican Council, who as a worker priest had mobilized youth and their idealism to action on behalf of social justice using this method. Pope John XXIII, in the encyclical *Mater et Magistra* (1961), had also aspired to energize the youth of his day to action for social justice by using this same approach.

Once an action plan begins, it is helpful to celebrate milestone achievements. This serves to strengthen the resolve of the participants and provides an opportunity to recruit more people. A scrapbook that documents the progress can be encouraging during inevitable setbacks.

As the plan is realized, evaluation is important. Here are some basic questions:

- What in the process went well?
- What did not go as well as planned?
- Were there steps that should have been included?
- What has been gleaned from this experience that will help when another issue of social justice needs to be addressed?
- Who has been impacted by this action step?
- Who still needs to be impacted or informed about the issue?
- Have lives been improved because of what has taken place?
- Does the completion of this action step lead to a need for further action?
- What systemic changes have been made?
- Is there a need to bring the issue(s) to the wider public?
- Are there key players in the community who need to be involved?
- Are there more resource people, within or outside the parish, who could significantly impact any implementation plans?

See–judge–act was instrumental to the cathedral community erecting its recent ministries. Some parishioners had observed refugees, recent arrivals to the cathedral neighborhood, on the street without protective winter covering. At the same time, the staff attended a meeting at city hall to see the extent of the refugee crisis and learned about this vulnerable population with growing needs, impacting the urban landscape (phase 1: "see").

We had been "served notice."

At the cathedral, the Catholic Family Center, a part of the local Catholic Charities, became the primary tool for critical analysis of needs and potential programming (phase 2: "judge"). One office of the center managed the program assisting refugees as they arrived. They could provide current data on the rate of arrivals, identification of the predominant source countries, and importantly, extensive information about immigration law. Resources limited their participation to the initial arrival and initial stages of refugee acclimation.

Phase 3, "to act," became picking up with the refugees where Catholic Charities ended. An outreach center (to be called Mary's Place) was founded to feed, cloth, tutor, and supply assistance with green cards and citizenship, as well as contribute advocacy for fair treatment in employment and against discrimination.

Similarly, Joseph's Place was launched after "observation"—the critical gaze at the neighborhood surrounding the cathedral community. The parish staff shared with the parish council the trauma they saw every day. The needs were severe. One need was food.

Critical analysis was provided by a local research project that had published alarming statistical evidence about the extent of urban poverty. The vast discrepancy between the "haves" and the "have-nots" was staggering. We also needed to examine and reflect on the Catholic social justice tradition. The Scriptures are replete with instructions about care for the poor, epitomized most starkly by Jesus in Matthew 25: "I was hungry and you gave me food" (v. 35). So, too, the Catholic social justice doctrine, based on scriptural teachings, forcefully demanded our concern for the "least of our brothers and sisters."

The "action" phase was the creation of Joseph's Place, a food pantry to augment the other local efforts to feed the poor of the neighborhood. The ministry continues to grow in supplying food for the increasing number of people that need to be fed and is expanding its services to target areas of systemic injustice.

"See–judge–act" has been a key methodology for our parish in proclaiming *The Joy of the Gospel* and the crucial parish definition provided by the U.S. bishops: "A parish cannot really proclaim the gospel if its message is not reflected in its own community life. The biblical call to charity, justice and peace claims not only each believer, but also each community where believers gather for worship, formation, and pastoral care."[2]

FOR REFLECTION AND DISCUSSION

1. In what ways can the "see–judge–act" paradigm integrate social justice with practical action?
2. What are the most prominent factors that prevent the initial observance, "the see" in our surroundings?
3. To gaze at the city, according to Pope Francis, is to see with a contemplative gaze, "God dwelling in homes," to see struggles, death, poverty—and light. How can our "gaze" best be directed to the issues that need to be further examined and addressed?
4. An important dynamic, while observing, is how what I see is affecting me personally. How does this relationship encourage proactivity toward a possible solution?
5. "To judge," according to this methodology, is to begin an analysis of what has been seen. What disciplines of the social sciences and theology would seem most appropriate for analyzing an issue brought to the attention of a parish or any faith community?
6. What resources can be utilized from the Christian tradition for a theological analysis of what has been seen and needs to be addressed?
7. "To act" is perhaps the most important of the three steps. How do we make sure that the action steps are viable and are within the realm of "reality"?

Chapter 9

A PEOPLE WITH A SPIRITED IMPULSE

> Without prolonged moments of adoration, of prayerful encounter with the word, of sincere conversation with the Lord, our work easily becomes meaningless; we lose energy as a result of weariness and difficulties, and our fervor dies out.

Evangelii Gaudium 262

Pope Francis urges the Church to reform its structures, a transformation that "cannot be delayed." As described in *The Joy of the Gospel*, change is urgent for the structure of the *parish*, whose contours of creative adaptability can stretch its purpose toward missionary discipleship. As a recent Vatican document describes, the parish is called to a new energy and vitality for missionary service: "It is necessary to identify perspectives that allow for the renewal of 'traditional' Parish structures in terms of mission. This is the heart of the desired pastoral conversion, which must touch the proclamation of the Word of God, the sacramental life and the witness of charity, in other words the essential areas in which the Parish grows and conforms to the Mystery in which it believes."[1] The recent coronavirus pandemic has had a devastating impact on the ability of the parish to function. In most dioceses, including my own, public celebration of Mass was suspended. Everyone was asked to "shelter in place," to stay home, and to avoid any unnecessary travel. Our parish, like many, maintained contact with the parish through a variety of means, most especially social media, including our website, Facebook, email, and other creative ways, including a twice-weekly e-newsletter. Masses were electronically broadcast, "livestreamed." But we received many letters, calls, or emails from parishioners about how much they missed gathering in community for the Eucharist. That communal experience—gathering, breaking open the Word and the Eucharist, and then setting out in mission—could not be replicated by viewing Mass on a screen. We hope that when we can all gather once again at the Lord's table, we will be strengthened in our appreciation of the weekly gathering by what we had missed in the lockdown and be renewed in energy and enthusiasm for missionary discipleship as Pope Francis has challenged us to be Church.

Pope Francis provides an integration of his vision for renewal concerning the structures of the Church and particularly of the parish as he concludes his apostolic exhortation with a section called "Spirit-Filled Evangelizers"—with a "Renewed Missionary Impulse."

The parish's mission flows from each member's encounter with the saving love of Jesus Christ. Believers, touched by the love of Jesus, as a community are nourished at the Eucharist, and then sent to proclaim what they have experienced.

Our ministry flows from our cognizance of the passionate love of Jesus Christ for us. We gaze at those whom we are called to serve, within and outside the parish church. Our gaze extends beyond those with whom we worship at the celebration of the Eucharist. Our cathedral community, after gazing at the bread of life in the breaking of the bread, began to gaze at the neighborhood—at the severe poverty—and there also saw Jesus.

Jesus preached his message with imagery readily grasped by his audience. The sower and seeds, mustard seeds, and the employer who hired workers late in the day yet gave them the same pay as he did to those who had begun work earlier resonated with his hearers. He had entered their life experiences and their struggles. They realized that this prophet and preacher understood why they suffered, why they were poor, and why they felt oppressed. He had entered into "the fabric of society." The cathedral community, when it organized Mary's Place for refugees and Joseph's Place for the neighborhood poor, could not begin until it had listened to needs, sometimes by direct conversation, sometimes by listening to experts and agencies, sometimes by an intensive grappling with social dynamics. Parishioners could not engage in ministry until they could "rejoice with those who rejoice, weep with those who weep" (Rom 12:15), rather than act from a moral obligation.

During the year, the parish had had a monthly collection called "The Penny Fund" to collect loose change for charitable assistance to organizations that had sent requests to the parish. A parish committee would review the solicitation letters, select the recipients, and send the checks. In some ways, however, this noble effort protected the parish from the "Lord's wounds"—keeping the afflicted individuals at arm's length and leaving the appropriate care to an agency. Pope Francis says, "Yet Jesus wants us to touch human misery, to touch the suffering flesh of others....Stop looking for those personal or communal niches which shelter us from the maelstrom of human misfortune and instead enter into the reality of other people's lives and know the power of tenderness" (*EG* 270). The Penny Fund developed into hands-on service. Now, the funding was directed toward our neighborhood. After completing a preliminary form detailing the specific assistance desired, our social ministries coordinator would sit with the applicant to review the form and provide some extended opportunity for gentle listening. Many who came were facing immediate eviction or the imminent loss of essential services. The ministry has been expanded with three parishioners, retired social workers, generous with their time, who are now meeting with the applicants and are able, based on their professional experience, to provide more timely referrals to agencies and other resources.

It's easy to see the continuous stream of people with complex, often life-or-death needs as "problems to be solved" and not as human beings with dignity who require pastoral ministry. It is difficult to deliver hope to these and other similar situations: a family with no food, a refugee family lacking housing, or a mother with several children arriving at our door with an eviction notice. "It is true that in our dealings with the world, we are told to give reasons for our hope, but not as an enemy who critiques and condemns. We are told quite clearly: 'do so with gentleness and reverence'" (*EG* 271). As we embrace our own humanity and the humanity of others, we appreciate how "wonderfully complicated" our lives are and "we experience intently what it is to be a people, to be part of a people" (*EG* 270). Any hope we provide comes not "as an enemy who critiques and condemns [as] grandees who look down upon others" but as men and women *of the people*. It is an indispensable approach not because it comes from any pope or because it provides a good pastoral option; rather, these are instructions from the word of God, "which are so clear, direct and convincing that they need no interpretation which might *diminish their power to challenge us*" (*EG* 271). The result of such an approach is joy: "We will know the missionary joy of sharing life with God's faithful people as we strive to light a fire in the heart of the world" (*EG* 271).

The spiritual life is inseparably linked to going outside of ourselves. "If we want to advance in the spiritual life, then we must constantly be missionaries," knowing the "joy of being a spring which spills over and refreshes others. Only the person who feels happiness in seeking the good of others, in desiring their happiness, can be a missionary" (*EG* 272). Powerful is the bond of the Christian inner life and the outward drive of the disciple: "We do not live better when we flee, hide, refuse to share, stop giving and lock ourselves up in our own comforts. Such a life is nothing less than slow suicide" (*EG* 272).

It is impossible to confine our missionary life to a specific time and place. "My mission of being in the heart of the people is not just a part of my life, or a badge I can take off; it is not an 'extra' or just another moment of life. Instead, it is something I cannot uproot from my being without destroying my very self" (*EG* 273). The parishioners who minister at Joseph's Place could find it easy to compartmentalize the time serving at the food pantry: preparing for the opening, the prayer of the ministers before the doors open, serving the guests, cleaning up, and locking the doors—"the ministry." It is finished until we reopen next week. *No!* "*I am a mission on this earth; that is why I am here in the world.* We have to regard ourselves as sealed, even branded, by this mission of bringing light, blessing, enlivening, raising up, healing and freeing" (*EG* 273). We become immersed in Jesus and our vision of life is radically changed. My prayer, my associations, my commitments—because of Jesus— are wholly integrated because I am "a new person in Christ." I cannot fold and place my mission neatly in a drawer like the apron I wear when distributing food to the poor. I am now clothed with Jesus Christ. Because you are "God's chosen ones, holy and beloved, clothe yourselves with compassion, kindness, humility, meekness, and patience" (Col 3:12), and that makes all the difference. "It is a wonderful thing to be God's faithful people," proclaims *The Joy of the Gospel.* "We achieve fulfillment when we break down walls and our heart is filled with faces and names" (*EG* 274).

This will not eliminate formidable pitfalls. When we began Mary's Place and Joseph's Place, we were not prepared for the numerous snags: quickly exhausting the food supply at the pantry, the flaring tempers of impatient guests, challenges at Mary's Place in communication with refugees, and the impatience in both sides in responding to the needs. "New difficulties are constantly surfacing; experiences of failure and the human weaknesses which bring so much pain. We all know from experience that sometimes a task does not bring the satisfaction we seek, results are few, changes are slow and we are tempted to grow weary" (*EG* 277). On more than one occasion the ministers at Joseph's Place would shake their heads: "Is this worth the trouble? What are we accomplishing? Why are we causing ourselves so much grief? Why did I get involved in such heartbreaking work?"

POPE FRANCIS AND THE PARISH

In Exodus 17:11–13, Moses required help in keeping his arms raised, which brought victory to the people, and he is helped in that task by others holding up his arms. At times our arms, heavy into ministry, grow weary, but there is a difference, according to the pope, in lowering our arms momentarily because we are tired, and in lowering them "for good" because we have become disillusioned, or discontent in the labor, with a certain listlessness. "Our hearts can tire of the struggle because in the end we are caught up in ourselves, in a careerism which thirsts for recognition, applause, rewards, and status. In this case we do not lower our arms, but we no longer grasp what we seek, the resurrection is not there. In cases like these, the Gospel, the most beautiful message that this world can offer, is buried under a pile of excuses" (*EG* 277).

The work of Joseph's Place has always seen the necessity of prayer and days of reflection. Before the actual distribution of food at Joseph's Place begins, the ministers gather for prayer, prepared by one of the workers, followed by reflection and intercession. Always included are prayers for the many benefactors of Joseph's Place, whose generosity finances the purchased food, but the opportunity to pause before the ministry to the guests begins helps us to remember why we are here and why we do what we do. It is not "our work" but the Lord's. We meditate on the "most beautiful message that the world can offer." It prevents us from seeing ourselves as "saviors," but instead as instruments. It can stem our human need for acknowledgment or praise. It also reminds us that the best thing we offer is Jesus Christ, best done by treating each guest with respect. This has often led to extraordinary conversations that display starkly our common humanity. Their struggles become ours by a common humanity; we need each other, and we depend on the grace of God.

Another frustration is not always seeing improvement. The same people are returning for help, and the poverty around us does not seem to improve. *The Joy of the Gospel* states, "Because we do not always see these seeds growing, we need an interior certainty, a conviction that God is able to act in every situation, even amid apparent setbacks"

(*EG* 279). For those days when nothing seems to bear fruit, we are reminded that "we may be sure that none of our acts of love for God will be lost, nor any of our acts of sincere concern for others. No single act of love for God will be lost, no generous effort is meaningless, no painful endurance is wasted. All of these encircle our world like a vital force" (*EG* 279). This vital force is powerful. Keeping our missionary fervor alive calls for firm trust in the Holy Spirit, for it is he who "helps us in our weakness" (Rom 8:26). This is not something that can be done once and then forgotten. This invoking of the Holy Spirit must be a constant, for he can heal when we flag in our endeavors. "There is no greater freedom than that of allowing oneself to be guided by the Holy Spirit, renouncing the attempt to plan and control everything to the last detail, and instead letting him enlighten, guide and direct us, leading us wherever he wills" (*EG* 280).

Pope Francis and *The Joy of the Gospel* pushes, cajoles, entices, and drives us forward and outward to get messy and dirty as missionary disciples. The kingdom of God is here and seeks always to flourish anew, with our help. "May we never remain on the sidelines of this march of living hope!" (*EG* 278).

FOR REFLECTION AND DISCUSSION

1. *The Joy of the Gospel* calls for a reform of Church structures, a reform that "cannot be delayed." Why are Church structures often difficult to reform? What might be involved in initial steps for structural reform?
2. An instruction issued by the Vatican Congregation for the Clergy says it "is necessary to identify perspectives that allow for the renewal of 'traditional' Parish structures in terms of mission." What are the ideal perspectives that enable a renewal and pastoral conversion to missionary discipleship?

3. The pope identifies the parish's mission with the encounter of its members with the saving love of Jesus. How can parish leadership best encourage and enhance that encounter and direct an outward impulse to the marginalized?

4. The pope carefully and emphatically reminds those who embark in missionary discipleship to do so with an appropriate attitude, to appreciate "what it is to be a people, to be part of a people." How does this perspective better enhance our efforts at discipleship?

5. What is the relationship, according to *The Joy of the Gospel*, between personal fulfillment and missionary discipleship?

6. "We do not live better when we flee, hide, refuse to share, stop giving and lock ourselves up in our own comforts. Such a life is nothing less than slow suicide." How is the bond of the Christian inner life connected best to the outward drive of the disciple?

7. How do we best balance the attempt to "plan and control everything to the last detail" in our missionary efforts with the guidance and direction of the Holy Spirit?

NOTES

PREFACE

1. John L. Allen Jr., "'Evangelii Gaudium' Amounts to Francis' 'I Have a Dream Speech,'" *National Catholic Reporter*, November 26, 2013, https://www.ncronline.org/news/theology/evangelii-gaudium -amounts-francis-i-have-dream-speech.

2. Pope Francis, apostolic exhortation *Evangelii Gaudium* (*The Joy of the Gospel*, November 24, 2013) (hereinafter cited in text as *EG* followed by the paragraph number), https://www.vatican .va/content/francesco/en/apost_exhortations/documents/papa -francesco_esortazione-ap_20131124_evangelii-gaudium.html.

3. Vatican Council II, Constitution on the Sacred Liturgy, *Sacrosanctum Concilium* (December 4, 1963), https://www.vatican .va/archive/hist_councils/ii_vatican_council/documents/vat-ii _const_19631204_sacrosanctum-concilium_en.html.

4. Vatican Council II, Decree on Ecumenism, *Unitatis Redintegratio* (November 21, 1964), https://www.vatican.va/archive/hist _councils/ii_vatican_council/documents/vat-ii_decree_19641121 _unitatis-redintegratio_en.html.

5. Vatican Council II, Decree on the Church's Missionary Activity, *Ad Gentes* (December 7, 1965), https://www.vatican.va/ archive/hist_councils/ii_vatican_council/documents/vat-ii_decree _19651207_ad-gentes_en.html.

CHAPTER 1

1. Austen Ivereigh, *The Great Reformer: Francis and the Making of a Radical Pope* (New York: Henry Holt, 2015), 57.

2. Chris Lowney, *Pope Francis: Why He Leads the Way He Leads: Lessons from the First Jesuit Pope* (Chicago: Loyola Press, 2013), 4.

3. Dushan Croos, *Pope Francis* (London: Ignatius Press, 2013), 16.

4. Croos, *Pope Francis*, 17.

5. Croos, *Pope Francis*, 17.

6. Ivereigh, *Great Reformer*, 111.

7. Ivereigh, *Great Reformer*, 111.

8. Ivereigh, *Great Reformer*, 117.

9. Antonio Spadaro, "A Big Heart Open to God," *Thinking Faith*, September 19, 2013, 6, https://www.thinkingfaith.org/sites/default/files/20130919_1.pdf.

10. Lowney, *Pope Francis*, 9.

11. Croos, *Pope Francis*, 27.

12. Ivereigh, *Great Reformer*, 239.

13. Ivereigh, *Great Reformer*, 239.

14. Ivereigh, *Great Reformer*, 262.

15. Ivereigh, *Great Reformer*, 9–10.

16. Ivereigh, *Great Reformer*, 2, 11.

17. Pope John XXIII, "Opening Speech to the Council," in *The Documents of Vatican II*, ed. Walter Abbott (New York: America Press, 1966), 716.

18. Pope John XXIII, "Opening Speech," 712.

19. Bradford Hinze, *Prophetic Obedience: Ecclesiology of a Dialogical Church* (Maryknoll, NY: Orbis Books, 2016), 3.

20. Hinze, *Prophetic Obedience*, 3.

21. Pope Paul VI, *Evangelii Nuntiandi* (On Evangelization on the Modern World), https://www.vatican.va/content/paul-vi/en/apost_exhortations/documents/hf_p-vi_exh_19751208_evangelii-nuntiandi.html.

22. Ivereigh, *Great Reformer*, 122.

23. Ivereigh, *Great Reformer*, 357.

24. Ivereigh, *Great Reformer*, 122.

25. Ivereigh, *Great Reformer*, 376.

26. Pope Paul VI, *Populorum Progressio* (On the Development of Peoples), https://www.vatican.va/content/paul-vi/en/encyclicals/documents/hf_p-vi_enc_26031967_populorum.html.

27. Thomas M. Kelly, *When the Gospel Grows Feet: An Ecclesiology in Context* (Collegeville, MN: Liturgical Press, 2013), 85.

28. Kelly, *When the Gospel Grows Feet*, 95.

29. Thomas Rourke, *The Roots of Pope Francis's Social and Political Thought: From Argentina to the Vatican* (New York: Rowman & Littlefield, 2016), 80.

30. Rourke, *Roots of Pope Francis's Thought*, 85.

31. Rourke, *Roots of Pope Francis's Thought*, 103.

32. Ivereigh, *Great Reformer*, 184.

33. Ivereigh, *Great Reformer*, 298.

34. Ivereigh, *Great Reformer*, 300.

35. Ivereigh, *Great Reformer*, 298.

36. Ivereigh, *Great Reformer*, 300.

CHAPTER 2

1. *Aparecida* Concluding Document 2 (hereinafter cited in text as *Aparecida*), accessed February 9, 2022, https://www.celam.org/aparecida/Ingles.pdf.

2. Pope Benedict XVI, *God Is Love* (Boston: Pauline Books and Media, 2006), 1.

3. Pope Benedict XVI, *Aparecida* Inaugural Address, 4.

4. Pope Benedict XVI, *God Is Love*, 15, 20.

5. John Chrysostom, *In Evangelium S. Matthaei*, homily 50:3–4, 58, 508–9.

6. Pope Benedict XVI, *Aparecida* Inaugural Address, 4.

7. Joseph Ratzinger, Conference given at the Meeting of Presidents of Bishops Commission of Latin America for the doctrine of the faith, held in Guadalajara (Mexico), 1996. Published in *L'Osservatore Romano*, November 1, 1996.

CHAPTER 4

1. Vatican Council II, *Lumen Gentium*, https://www.vatican.va/archive/hist_councils/ii_vatican_council/documents/vat-ii_const_19641121_lumen-gentium_en.html.

2. Pope Paul VI, *Evangelii Nuntiandi* (On Evangelization on the Modern World), https://www.vatican.va/content/paul-vi/en/apost_exhortations/documents/hf_p-vi_exh_19751208_evangelii-nuntiandi.html.

CHAPTER 5

1. Antonio Spadaro, "A Big Heart Open to God," *Thinking Faith*, September 19, 2013, 7, https://www.thinkingfaith.org/articles/20130919_1.htm.

2. See Joseph Kelly, "Heal the Wounds: Best Practices for the Church as Field Hospital," *America*, March 17, 2014, 18–21, https://www.americamagazine.org/issue/%E2%80%98heal-wounds%E2%80%99.

CHAPTER 6

1. William Werpehowski, "The Social Vision of *The Joy of the Gospel*," in *Pope Francis and the Future of Catholicism:* Evangelii Gaudium *and the Papal Agenda*, ed. Gerard Mannion (New York: Cambridge University Press, 2017), 125–42.

2. Edward Doherty, "Poverty and the Concentration of Poverty in the Nine-County Greater Rochester Area" (Rochester, NY: Act Rochester/The Community Foundation, 2013).

3. Pope Francis, *Laudato Si': On Care for Our Common Home*, https://www.vatican.va/content/francesco/en/encyclicals/documents/papa-francesco_20150524_enciclica-laudato-si.html.

CHAPTER 8

1. Adapted from "Reading the Signs of the Times: See, Judge, Act: A Process for Social Justice Groups," Australian Catholic Social Justice Council, https://socialjustice.catholic.org.au.

2. United States Conference of Catholic Bishops, *Communities of Salt and Light: Reflections on the Social Mission of the Parish*, rev. ed. (Washington, DC: USCCB Communications, 2006), 4.

CHAPTER 9

1. Congregation for the Clergy, "Instruction: The Pastoral Conversion of the Parish Community in the Service of the Evangelizing Mission of the Church," July 20, 2020, 20, https://press.vatican.va/content/salastampa/en/bollettino/pubblico/2020/07/20/200720a.html.

SOURCES

Abbot, Walter M., ed. *The Documents of Vatican II.* New York: America Press, 1966.

Allen, John L., Jr. *Against the Tide: The Radical Leadership of Pope Francis.* Liguori, MO: Liguori, 2014.

Aparecida Document. V General Conference of the Bishops of Latin America, May 13–31, 2007. https://www.celam.org/aparecida/Ingles.pdf.

Australian Catholic Social Justice Council. "Reading the Signs of the Times." https://socialjustice.catholic.org.au.

Benedict XVI (pope). *God Is Love.* Boston: Pauline Books and Media, 2006. https://www.vatican.va/content/benedict-xvi/en/encyclicals/documents/hf_ben-xvi_enc_20051225_deus-caritas-est.html.

Brennan, Patrick. *Re-Imagining the Parish.* New York: Crossroad, 1990.

Cleary, Edward L. *How Latin America Saved the Soul of the Catholic Church.* New York: Paulist Press, 2009.

Croos, Dushan. *Pope Francis.* London: Ignatius Press, 2013.

Doherty, Edward. "Poverty and the Concentration of Poverty in the Nine-County Greater Rochester Area." Rochester, NY: Act Rochester/The Community Foundation, 2013.

Dormor, Duncan, and Alana Harris, eds. *Pope Francis:* Evangelii Gaudium, *and the Renewal of the Church.* Mahwah, NJ: Paulist Press, 2017.

Editors, The. "A Lesson from Pope Francis: Evangelizing Through Pastoral Accompaniment." *America,* June 1, 2017. https://www

.americamagazine.org/faith/2017/06/01/lesson-pope-francis
-evangelizing-through-pastoral-accompaniment.

Faggioli, Massimo. *Pope Francis: Tradition in Transition.* Mahwah,
NJ: Paulist Press, 2015.

Francis (pope). Address on the Vigil of Pentecost to the Ecclesial
Movements, May 18, 2013. https://www.vatican.va/content/
francesco/en/speeches/2013/may/documents/papa-francesco
_20130518_veglia-pentecoste.html.

————. Address to Workers, Largo Carlo Felice, Cagliari, Sardinia,
September 22, 2013. https://www.vatican.va/content/frances
co/en/speeches/2013/september/documents/papa-francesco
_20130922_lavoratori-cagliari.html.

————. *Disciples Together on the Road: Words of Pope Francis for
Priests.* Vatican City: Libreria Editrice Vaticana, 2016.

————. *Evangelii Gaudium (The Joy of the Gospel)*, November 24,
2018. https://www.vatican.va/content/francesco/en/apost_exhor
tations/documents/papa-francesco_esortazione-ap_20131124
_evangelii-gaudium.html.

————. *Gaudete et Exsultate* (Rejoice and Be Glad: On the Call
to Holiness in Today's World), March 19, 2018. https://
www.vatican.va/content/francesco/en/apost_exhortations/
documents/papa-francesco_esortazione-ap_20180319
_gaudete-et-exsultate.html.

————. Homily, Salina Quarter, Lampedusa, July 8, 2013.
https://www.vatican.va/content/francesco/en/homilies/2013/
documents/papa-francesco_20130708_omelia-lampedusa
.html.

————. *I Ask You, Be Shepherds: Reflections on Pastoral Ministry.*
Translated by Michael O'Hearn. New York: Crossroad, 2015.

————. *Laudato Si'* (On Care for Our Common Home), May 24,
2015. https://www.vatican.va/content/francesco/en/encyclicals/
documents/papa-francesco_20150524_enciclica-laudato-si.html.

Ivereigh, Austen. *The Great Reformer: Francis and the Making of a
Radical Pope.* New York: Henry Holt, 2015.

John XXIII (pope). *Mater et Magistra* (Mother and Teacher), May 15, 1961. https://www.vatican.va/content/john-xxiii/en/encyclicals/documents/hf_j-xxiii_enc_15051961_mater.html.

———. *Pacem in Terris* (Peace on earth), April 11, 1963. https://www.vatican.va/content/john-xxiii/en/encyclicals/documents/hf_j-xxiii_enc_11041963_pacem.html.

John Paul II (pope). Post-synodal apostolic exhortation *Ecclesia in Oceania* (November 22, 2001), *AAS* 94 (2002). https://www.vatican.va/content/john-paul-ii/en/apost_exhortations/documents/hf_jp-ii_exh_20011122_ecclesia-in-oceania.html.

Kelly, Thomas M. *When the Gospel Grows Feet: An Ecclesiology in Context.* Collegeville, MN: Liturgical Press, 2013.

Lowney, Chris. *Pope Francis: Why He Leads the Way He Leads: Lessons from the First Jesuit Pope.* Chicago: Loyola Press, 2013.

Mannion, Gerard, ed. *Pope Francis and the Future of Catholicism: Evangelii Gaudium and the Papal Agenda.* New York: Cambridge University Press, 2017.

Massaro, Thomas. *Catholic Social Teaching in Action: Living Justice.* Classroom edition. New York: Rowman & Littlefield, 2008.

Paul VI (pope). *Evangelii nuntiandi* (On Evangelization in the Modern World), December 8, 1975. https://www.vatican.va/content/paul-vi/en/apost_exhortations/documents/hf_p-vi_exh_19751208_evangelii-nuntiandi.html.

Rauschenberg, Thomas P., and Richard R. Gaillardetz, eds. *Go into the Streets: The Welcoming Church of Pope Francis.* Mahwah, NJ: Paulist Press, 2016.

Rolheiser, Ronald. *The Holy Longing: The Search for Christian Spirituality.* New York: Doubleday, 1999.

Rourke, Thomas. *The Roots of Pope Francis's Social and Political Thought: From Argentina to the Vatican.* New York: Rowman & Littlefield, 2016.

Ruddy, Christopher. "Responses to Synod 2014: A Journey of Accompaniment," October 27, 2014. https://www.america

magazine.org/content/all-things/responses-synod-2014
-journey-accompaniment.

Sweetser, Thomas. *Keeping the Covenant: Taking Parish to the Next Level.* New York: Crossroad, 2007.

Tornielli, Andrea, and Giacomo Galeazzi. *This Economy Kills: Pope Francis on Capitalism and Social Justice.* Translated by Demetrio S. Yocum. Collegeville, MN: Liturgical Press, 2015.

Twenty-Third Ordinary General Assembly of the Synod of Bishops, October 7–28, 2012. The New Evangelization for the Transmission of the Christian Faith.

Ulrich, Tom. *Strategies for Success: Parish Social Ministry.* Notre Dame, IN: Ave Maria Press, 2001.

Vatican Council II. *Constitutions, Decrees, Declarations.* Austin Flannery, ed. Northport, NY: Costello Publishing, 1996.